ISBN 978-1-330-88176-7
PIBN 10116547

Similar Books Are Available from
www.forgottenbooks.com

Rutland Barrington

A Record of Thirty-five Years' Experience
on the English Stage

By
Himself

With a Preface by
Sir William S. Gilbert

With Thirty-two Illustrations
from Photographs

London
Grant Richards
1908

The Picture on the Cover is reproduced from
a Drawing by Mr. C. V. Bridgman

235 8744 B

Ref. Hassnitz

Wr~

PRINTED BY
WILLIAM BRENDON AND SON, LTD.
BY

Dedication

To my very good friend Mrs. D'Oyly Carte,
to whose consideration and kindly thought
for the comfort of all and sundry in
her employ, is due the maintenance of the best tradition
of the Savoy, that of
" A Happy Family."

Author's Note

WISH to acknowledge my indebtedness to Sir William S. Gilbert, not only for his kindness in supplying a Foreword to my book, but also for the self - imposed task of reading the proofs and pointing out certain errors.

If it should be my misfortune in the following pages to wound in the slightest degree the feelings of any person I may have alluded to, I humbly implore all such persons to believe that it has been done quite inadvertently.

Foreword

I HAVE been asked by my old friend Mr. Rutland Barrington to write a few words of introduction to his volume of reminiscences. I should have thought that he could do this for himself more effectively than I could do it for him, but perhaps he has formed such a modest estimate of his personal and professional claims to consideration that he is unwilling to draw a bill upon public attention unless his draft is, so to speak, " backed " by one who is in a position to testify to the fact that he is a man of undoubted substance. His action in the matter must be referable either to this motive or to an underlying principle, never to do for himself that which he can induce any one to do for him. Personally, I am disposed to believe that both of these influences may be involved.

The private identity of a popular actor is, undoubtedly, an object of infinite curiosity to the general body of playgoers who, having known him for many years under a plurality of physical and moral disguises, are naturally curious to know how he looks, acts, and thinks, when he is playing the leading part in the comedy, drama, tragedy, or farce of his own existence. I was myself the slave of this particular form of curiosity until it was extinguished by familiar intercourse with many distinguished members of the profession. I remember that when I was a boy of thirteen I followed Mr. Tom Barry (the then well-known clown at Astley's Amphitheatre) all the way from Temple Bar to Westminster Bridge, trying to make up my mind to ask him the time. Unfortunately, however, just as I had screwed up my courage to the sticking point, Mr. Barry baffled me by turning suddenly into a public house of refreshment, whither I had not the enterprise to follow him. I may state that I have long given up the practice of shadowing clowns.

Mr. Rutland Barrington's claims upon public attention are so numerous and so generally recognized that the incidents of his professional career, his private life, and his personal opinion on men and things, are sure to prove attractive and interesting to that vast body of his admirers who never see him except with a row of footlights between him and them. They know nothing of his performance in one of the best of his parts—certainly the longest—*himself;* and this volume reveals its many delightful characteristics. His native geniality, good humour, and sense of fun—qualities to which no one can testify more authoritatively than I—find kindred expression in a book which is eloquent both of the man and his methods.

W. S. GILBERT.

Contents

9

CONTENTS

List of Illustrations

I

EARLY ACTING—BANKING—THE OLYMPIC— ENTERTAINMENT

I WONDER if any notable person who has ventured on the task of setting forth in print reminiscences extending over many years, without the assistance of any notes or diaries, has approached the task with the same nervous dread and ignorance of the magnitude of the undertaking as I felt when embarking on my voyage of discovery—for such it will truly have been. Hours have been devoted to unearthing the treasures of memory, many of which have, on inspection, been rejected as paste. The kindly criticism of the Press, even on those rare occasions when it was adverse (for having kept all my "notices" I am able to administer an occasional cold douche to my vanity), has to a certain extent encouraged me to write this book, while at the same time inspiring a kind of fear that I may fail to reach the literary standard demanded of bookmakers, even when they only wish to amuse. Of course, the sordid or commercial point of view is also alluring. I find it very difficult to avoid the constant use of the personal pronoun in writing what is, I suppose, an autobiography, and yet there are a number of people who seem to expect it of you. I have already experienced this, as when writing a few reminiscences some years ago, in the shape of weekly articles, I received one day at my club an anonymous letter to the effect that "if you said a good deal less about yourself and more about other people it would be more amusing and show less conceit."

My first appearance as an actor took place, as with very many others doubtless, in the T.R. Backdrawing-room, when I gave an early demonstration of future ability by playing two parts in the one piece, this being a musical and dramatic version of a then popular song called "Home they brought her Warrior dead." I first played the warrior, covered with white antimacassars, which served later as gown and apron for my second part, a nurse of ninety years. Amongst our audience in those days (*circa* 1862) were two ladies who were then making name and fame for themselves ; the one, my dear aunt Emily Faithfull, being the pioneer of the movement for the employment of women, a cause to which she devoted her whole life and energy with such pronounced success ; and the other, Florence Marryat, the novelist, one of the most genial and delightful women I ever met, though I naturally did not discover this until I grew somewhat older.

This delay in appreciation did not arise entirely from a failure to understand the charm of the sex at so early an age, as I well remember being engaged at thirteen and painfully surprised at the attitude of the

MYSELF, ÆTAT. 7.

lady's father in absolutely refusing to look upon the affair as serious. This early portrait of me was taken at about the period of the warrior aforesaid, and many of my friends profess to discover in it traces of that calm demeanour without which Pooh Bah and the Rajah of Bhong would have been no more than ordinary mortals. This may well be so, but that calm was rudely shaken on the occasion of my next essay at acting, in the dear old Amateur Dramatic Club. I was cast for a non-speaking part. Did I refuse it? No; I played it and resigned. The club is defunct. Let this be a warning to other clubs.

After this my histrionic tendencies and abilities remained in abeyance until I came of age. They were also perhaps somewhat damped by a short career in the City, which finished with a period I can never recall without a shudder, namely, the infliction of eighteen months in a bank which was connected in some mysterious way with tea and India, but not, as far as I could discover, in any way with money. I know I got very little, and I am sure deserved less.

But now was to come the change that shaped my career in the way I had longed for. Through the kind offices of my dearly loved aunt, Emily Faithfull, I obtained an opening at the Olympic Theatre, then under the management of my good guide, philosopher, and friend, Henry Neville, and my first task was to understudy Luigi Lablache in *Lady Clancarty;* and at length, owing to some cause which at this lapse of time I forget, and which I was probably too excited to care about, I was told that I had to appear. When my cue came I had to speak "off" before making my entrance, and speak loudly, moreover. Could I do it? Not if my life had depended on it. I just whispered the line with a dry throat, walked on, and forgot all the rest!

Neville's kindly hand on my shoulder and a whispered word of encouragement brought me to myself, and all was well; but I have often wondered whether the audience noticed anything. Many strange things have happened to me on the stage since then, and I know now that audiences do not notice as much as you might suppose they would, though they almost invariably see what you would rather they did not.

My colleagues in this play were, in addition to Neville, Harcourt, Anson, Crichton (the father of Madge of comic opera fame), Walter Fisher, Ada Cavendish, and Emily Fowler, one of the most delightful soubrettes that ever graced the stage; and I had only one regret during the run, which was that I was executed after about two acts, and so had no excuse for staying longer in the society of people I admired so much. My next part was that of a waiter in the *Ticket of Leave Man*, and he was very important, though wordless, having to serve all the prominent characters with drinks, at a given cue, in the Cremorne Gardens scene.

Charles Harcourt and G. W. Anson played Hawk_

Photograph : The London Stereoscopic Co.

MY FIRST PART · SIR GEORGE BARCLAY, IN "CLANCARTY."

shaw and Jem Dalton respectively in this production, and having a wait during the evening of about an hour and a half, would frequently occupy it in rushing round to the Savage Club for a rubber or two. One night the rubber took longer to play than they thought, with the result that there was a dreadful hiatus in the play, presently filled by two breathless artists with no make-up and the wrong clothes on, who tumbled on to the stage and very nearly played the wrong scene. After this Neville prohibited going out during working hours, and presented the green-room with a box of dominoes. We enjoyed this game for some time, but Charles Sugden eventually became too clever for us all, and dominoes were " off."

I had a lesson in manners from one of the ladies of the company, in the green-room, for which I laid myself out in all innocence. Not being wanted till late, I used to come there first for a chat, and noticing the actors present wearing their hats, omitted to remove mine, which was done for me rather forcibly by the lady in question. It appeared, on my remonstrating, that costume hats may always be worn, outdoor ones not. It appeared to me at the time a foolish distinction, but of course is not so.

The next production was *The Two Orphans*, an adaptation from the French—a most stirring melodrama, containing one of the finest fights I ever saw on the stage. Henry Neville and William Rignold were the combatants, and the latter being a very big-

B

framed man and Neville slight, and also playing the part of a lame younger brother (the hero to the elder one's brute), it was very thrilling and most satisfactory to find the bully get his deserts. One night during the progress of this duel to the death there was a great commotion in the pit, caused, as we learned afterwards, by a poor woman who had been seriously ill for some time from melancholia. Her doctor had advised a visit to the theatre by way of cheering her up, but neglected to prescribe any particular one. She therefore chose for herself the play she would go to, and it finished her, for the poor soul never spoke after they carried her out. It is really never wise to go to a theatre when feeling depressed, there being quite enough risks in ordinary life.

Emily Fowler, who played the blind heroine, was extremely kind to me during my stay at the Olympic, and we remained good friends long after she retired from the stage, though we only met once a year on the roof-stalls of the grand stand on Derby Day.

For some three months of my engagement at the Olympic I was not particularly popular with my colleagues, in spite of all efforts to conciliate and please, and I could not understand why. However, after the aforesaid apprenticeship I was told I was to receive a salary, and my first appearance at "treasury" was the signal for the removal of all hostile feeling. I had been regarded, so it appeared, as a gilded interloper. Never shall I forget my feeling of pride when I drew my first week's salary—twelve shillings — at which figure it remained for about another three months, and I honestly believe I was worth it.

In *The Two Orphans* it was again my fate to be killed very early in the evening, but this time I did not regret it, as owing to the kindness of Henry Irving and Bateman I had the run of the Lyceum theatre, and after I had perished by the sword of Charles Sugden I would rush off to see Irving in his wonderful performance of *The Bells*.

Apropos Irving, I shall not easily forget my surprise when I was first introduced to him at a soirée given by Emily Faithfull at Norfolk Square, and found him to be a man of by no means great stature. I could not help wondering by what means he dominated the stage on which he appeared, and absolutely dwarfed men taller than himself. I was still young enough not to be aware that the art of the individual can add cubits to the stature.

Within a month or two of my first appearance on the stage I had an experience which I met with an aplomb which I should doubt my capacity to display now, for the reason that it sprang from the courage of ignorance. I had a scene in *The Two Orphans* in which my employer, the wicked Marquis, had to describe to me the appearance of a girl he wished carried off, give instructions where she was to be taken to, and finally point her out as she made her entrance. One night he failed to

answer to his cue to come on to me. I walked to
the wings and said, "Where is Mr. Roland? He ought
to be on." Some one rushed up to his dressing-room,
to return immediately with the news that he could
not possibly come, having taken off all his costume
to get ready for the second act (it seems he had
completely forgotten this short scene). Next I saw
Neville's anxious face at the side. I considered the
situation for a moment, then walked to the centre
and made a long speech combining his lines and
my replies, and then calmly walked off, to be received as little less than a hero by Neville, who said
he himself could not have done it! I rather wondered at this at the time, but I understand it better
now.

There were one or two more plays in which I
appeared at the Olympic, notably one by James
Albery, of which I forget the title, full of fancy and
quaint conceit; but I did not remain there very long
before joining a preparatory school for the Savoy.
Of course, I was not aware that it was so at the
time, but I recognized it as such later on. I allude
to my lengthy experience of "Entertainment" under
the banner of Mrs. Howard Paul.

What an experience it was, and what an invaluable schooling—seven changes of costume a night,
seven changes of make-up, seven changes of character to portray, and only six changes of town to
play them in! This sounds as if you could not get
them all in, but we did, and life was composed of

hurried meals, railway journeys, acting, and a little sleep.

Some of the journeys were truly awful, for in those days there was no railway company that possessed rolling-stock half as good as the now discarded Metropolitan trains. Mrs. Paul used to give a marvellously lifelike imitation of Sims Reeves, being the possessor of a voice with a quite abnormal range; indeed, it more nearly resembled two voices—a mezzo-soprano and pure tenor. She told me herself that on one occasion when engaged for the contralto music in an oratorio she sang that and also deputized for Sims Reeves, who was ill.

Of course, in our entertainment she assumed male evening dress, and wore a wig and moustache, the resemblance to the great tenor being so close as to be almost uncanny. We used to conclude the evening with a duet, I being made up as Santley (more or less of a libel, and quite so as regarded the voice), and it speaks well for the friendship between Santley and myself that he has never referred to this imitation. I have my suspicion that he saw it, which makes his silence the more noble. We carried what was known as a " fit-up " in those days, which in our case consisted of a kind of screen of heavy claret-coloured velvet curtains arranged on iron supports, which could be accommodated to any size of stage, and very funny were some of the stages in the town halls of the provinces in those bygone days. I remember that at Barmouth we struck something unusually small, and for dressing-rooms had to steal a small section from either side.   Mrs. Paul, in her character in the first sketch we were playing, had to bewail my delay in arriving to help her, interspersed with a few complimentary remarks referring to my talent.   Of course I could hear every word, and the audience knew I could hear, so I could not resist the temptation to say loudly, " Be careful, I can hear all you say."   I believe it secured the biggest laugh of the evening.   I also appeared, among other characters, as a member of the gentler sex, and discussed the affairs of the nation with Mrs. Paul, as two old maids; but for some reason or other, possibly the unaccustomed draperies, I felt oppressed and unhappy in the part, and very shortly ceased to be womanly in appearance.   What strange little places we used to visit, and, I rather fancy, coin money in too.   Even to this day, when an important Sunday special stops at some wayside station either to let something pass or give the engine a drink, it seems to me that I know the place, have been there, and perhaps helped to give one bright evening to the local rustics, some of whom are now leaning on a gate and looking at us in the superior way these people usually affect.   I feel quite friendly towards them, perhaps venture on some kind of pleasant greeting, and as often as not am met with a stony stare, or worse ; then I think I really must have played there.   During my engagement with Mrs. Paul came the incident which was to determine

Photograph   North London Photographic Co

MISS ALATHEA, IN MRS. HOWARD PAUL'S ENTERTAINMENT.

my future. She had been for some time in communication with D'Oyly Carte, who was very anxious to secure her for the part of Lady Sangazure in *The Sorcerer*, which was the first of the notable series of Gilbert and Sullivan operas produced under his management. She was quite willing to play the part, but my contract with her had still some time to run, and as she also wished to do me a service she informed Carte that I also must be provided with a part if she joined him. Carte agreed, subject of course to the approval of Gilbert, and on a momentous never-to-be-forgotten day Gilbert held a personal inspection of my charms and qualifications.

The vacant part was the important one of Doctor Daly, better known after the production as The Vicar, and a fact that seemed to have a certain amount of weight with Gilbert was that my father was very nearly a clergyman; he was, in fact, brought up for the Church, but through unforeseen circumstances was compelled to adopt the City as a career. I have no doubt that Gilbert reasoned that my inherited manner might be a valuable asset in the part of Doctor Daly; his judgment has always been extremely sound, and even my natural modesty confesses that the sequel once again proved it to be correct. To the best of my recollection, I was not called upon to display my vocal acquirements to Sullivan, which perhaps was as well.

I left town with the well-described feeling of treading on air, and full of a natural impatience for the entertainment tour to end and for the opportunity of turning my attention to what I considered serious acting.

Mrs. Paul was also, I fancy, rather pleased at the prospect of settling down for a time after so many weeks of wandering, more especially as she quite anticipated great pleasure as well as great success in her part. It was originally intended that she should also appear (in the same piece) as Ahrimanes in the second act, conjured up unwittingly by the Sorcerer, but for some reason this idea was abandoned and the part cut out, much to her disappointment at the time and relief later on.

II

In the autumn of 1877, shortly after the momentous interview alluded to in the last chapter, behold me, passed by the great author, rehearsing the part of Doctor Daly at the old Opera Comique theatre, now only a memory. My first appearance in London in a musical piece, and its title *The Sorcerer*—and what a prophetic title too, except that it should have been in the plural, for indeed two sorcerers had arisen to bewitch the ears of the public. And now think of this, some of ye modern actors who own motor-cars and palaces in Park Lane or Pimlico, I made the initial success of my career in one of the most important parts in a comic opera for the stupendous stipend of six pounds per week. Moreover, having made the success, I did not immediately clamour for better terms, and equally strange to relate, the management did not offer them. I do not wish for a moment to imply that I was more exceptionally cheap than the other artists of the company, which included my dear old colleague George Grossmith, jun. (as he was then); Bentham, a tenor who came, I believe, from Covent Garden opera; Richard Temple, Alice May, Giulia Warwick, Fred Clifton, and, as I

have said, Mrs. Howard Paul.   I have a shrewd suspicion that the all-round average would not have run
to much over double figures. What halcyon days for
managements! and who can wonder at the fortunes
amassed, and justly, by the great triumvirate? for
after all they took a certain risk in letting loose on
London a band of artists some of whom had never
before been heard of.

For the matter of that, none knew very much
about Gilbert and Sullivan except for the wonderful
success of their cantata, *Trial by Jury*, which had
shortly before this amazed and delighted London
with the brilliancy and humour of both words and
music, although even then it was impossible to guess
that this amusing little opera would become as it has
a fixed planet, so to speak, in the world of wit and
humour.   In proof of this, witness the way it shone
some short time since at Drury Lane in honour of
Ellen Terry's jubilee of work. Quite a notable feature
of this particular performance was the excellent
restrained force displayed in the part of the Associate
by the talented author of the libretto, who met with
a reception at the hands of the vast audience which
must have given him intense pleasure, as indicative
of the delight felt at yet one more opportunity of
manifesting the keen appreciation of the many hours
of fun his work has furnished.

In saying that no one knew very much about
Gilbert and Sullivan, I mean, of course, in their
capacity as a "Firm," for all the world had been

for long enjoying their work as individuals, the
musical status of Sullivan being already established,
while Gilbert, apart from plays he had written and
slight pieces for the German Reeds, had already en-
deared himself to all lovers of humour with the
famous "Bab Ballads"; but to my mind much of this
was overlooked when they took us all by storm as
"Gilbert and Sullivan." Say it aloud, and see how
it runs off the tongue. Truly it was a musical firm.
My goodness, how we all stood in awe of them at
the early rehearsals of the *Sorcerer!* We had not
had time to arrive at the kindly kernel concealed
beneath the autocratic exterior of the partners. Not
that the two together were then so autocratic as
one of them became later on. And good reason
they had too, for they dominated the musical
market, and to get with Gilbert, Sullivan, and
Carte was the one desire of every artist with or
without a voice.

The great initial idea was that every soul and
every thing connected with the venture should be
English. It was to be a home of English talent,
and so strong was this feeling that two choristers,
whose names were never likely to appear on the
programme, renounced their Italian titles and became Englishmen for the express purpose of being
associated with such an enterprise; and one dear
old fellow (he is still alive, though he seemed old
even then) very nearly missed his engagement
because his name was Parris. This sentiment in-

spired us all with a kind of patriotic glow combined with a determination to show other nations
(and *inter alia* our own) what we could do ; and
I remember feeling great distress at the risk run
by my old colleague Dick Temple, who would use
the "Italian production," which unfortunately there
was no mistaking. However, I was soothed by
noticing that it gradually left him during the course
of rehearsals.

I need hardly say how more than delighted I was
with my part ; I could not very well have a better
one offered me to-day. But as the time of production drew near I began to feel rather anxious about
it, and confessed as much one day to Gilbert, saying that I felt what a daring experiment it was to
introduce a Dean into comic opera, and that I
fancied the public would take either very kindly to me
or absolutely hoot me off the stage for ever. He
was very sympathetic, but his reply, " I quite agree
with you," left me in a state of uncertainty.

There was a song in the second act demanding
an obbligato on the flageolet, which Sullivan suggested should be played in the orchestra ; but I
demurred to that, and received permission to play
it for myself. A part was written out for me, I
learnt it (it was only two notes), and it added
enormously to the success of the song.

The Opera Comique, though giving from the
auditorium a sense of elegance and plenty of room,
was in reality one of the most cramped theatres it

Photograph   The London Stereoscopic Company

DR. DALY, IN "THE SORCERER."

has ever been my lot to play in. It was like a rabbit-warren for entrances, having three or four in as many different streets, and from the principal one, which was in the Strand, there was an excessively long and narrow tunnel to traverse before arriving at the stalls, which would have been an awful place in case of fire or any panic; fortunately the former never happened, and the latter only once, when it was speedily dissipated. With the exception of one or two little cabins, more resembling stoke-holes, below the level of the stage, occupied by the ladies and the tenor (I do not mean jointly, of course), all the dressing-rooms were upstairs, in houses along Holywell Street, commanding a fine view of the celebrated literary emporiums of those days, and reached from the stage by a flight of some thirty very steep stone steps, commencing almost at the street door. The back wall of the stage was also the back wall of that of the Globe Theatre; indeed, by placing the ear to any little crevice the players on either side could overhear the others.

George Grossmith, Richard Temple, Fred Clifton, and myself shared one not too large room, and George and I had to assert ourselves on one or two occasions in order to maintain an equality with the two older hands; but we were a very harmonious four for a long time, though there was nearly a split in the camp when Clifton insisted on supping in the dressing-room, our objection to which habit arose

entirely through his inordinate predilection for
sheep's head, possibly a very succulent dish, but a
truly ghastly object to look at. I believe it was a
supper much affected by "the old school," of which
he was undoubtedly a very talented member.

At last we arrived at the first night, and though
we all felt confident of success, we little dreamed
how this evening was to be the precursor of all those
historical first nights which remain without parallel
in the annals of our stage. I believe we were none
of us as nervous as we ought to have been, simply
for the reason that we hardly appreciated the magnitude of our undertaking. I can only say that personally I have felt very much more anxious at later first
nights. What a rush there was on the part of the
company for the next day's papers, and how eagerly
they were scanned! Really there are few sensations
much more pleasant than that of reading something
nice about yourself in print. I do not mind admitting
that it comes almost as fresh to me in 1908 as it did
in 1877. I will confess to a certain feeling of disappointment at the dictum of one well-known critic
of those days (whom later on I met and liked immensely), who said, " Barrington is perfectly wonderful. He always manages to sing about one-sixteenth
of a tone flat ; it's so like a vicar." As a matter of
fact, he was so pleased with this criticism that he was
constantly repeating it, with the ultimate result that
I established a reputation for doing it, and many
months later nearly got into trouble over it. Carte

himself came round to see me in a great state of mind, saying, "B., what's the matter?" I had visions of an ignominious dismissal for something, I did not know what, that I had done. "What is it, D'Oyly?" I said. "Why, some one has just come out of the stalls to tell me you are singing in tune. It will never do." This pleased me so much that I have never sung flat since, except, of course, when I wished, and in thus altering my method I unconsciously ruined an imitation of me which Charlie Hawtrey used to give, and which depended greatly on that sixteenth, though he was not particular to one.

I was much impressed with the thoughtfulness displayed by an unimportant member of the company, who would come nightly to inquire after the health of George Grossmith, and I told George how nice I thought it was of him. George quite agreed, but remarked parenthetically, "He's my understudy, you know, and he said he thought I was looking awfully overworked and in need of a change." I still maintained that I thought it very considerate behaviour, but when, later on, he offered George his expenses to go away for a few days, I began to think he was not quite so disinterested.

I believe that George Grossmith's quaint run round the stage, brandishing the teapot in which he had mixed the love-charm, was an absolutely unrehearsed effect; but whether this was so or not, the success of it was undeniable, and I imagine started the series of similar antics in the parts which followed, and without which he would have seemed rather at a loss.

The Sorcerer was memorable to me for one very personal reason, being the first play my father had ever seen. He had the old-fashioned, much **exaggerated** ideas of the wickedness of "life in the green-room," and indeed carried his convictions to the extent of saying that if I appeared on the boards (they called it the boards then) before I was of age, he would have me forcibly removed by the police. I do not know whether he could have done it, but I waited the prescribed time, and the dear old man softened so rapidly that within two years he found himself in a theatre looking at his son acting; and most complimentary he was to me.

After about one year of the church I launched on a seafaring career as the captain of *H.M.S. Pinafore*, which first saw the light in 1878. Surely this is one of the most joyous and breezy plays ever seen or likely to be. It is almost a cure for depression to whistle the first bars of the opening chorus, with its lilt so redolent of the sea. It is perfectly unaccountable, and yet the fact, that this opera did not take hold half so readily as *The Sorcerer* had; indeed, not until it had been produced in America, where our cousins went literally crazy over it, and the fame of it had travelled back to London, was it the success it eventually proved.

Jessie Bond made her first appearance in this opera as the leading relative of Sir Joseph Porter. She

CAPTAIN CORCORAN, IN "H.M S. PINAFORE." (ACT II) REVIVAL.

struck me at rehearsal as being of a rather stodgy, not over-intelligent type of girl, showing very few signs of the strong personality and great artistic capabilities that were to make her a firm favourite of the public within a short time. We had a change of tenor for this opera, Bentham being considered on too large a scale for Ralph Rackstraw, I believe, so that the new draft also included George Power, the possessor of a sweet if delicate voice, and a manner somewhat to match. He was suffering one night from a cold, and had played almost through the first act under difficulties when the finale came. It begins by Rackstraw rushing on to summon his friends with "Messmates ahoy!" Power's voice cracked very badly, and he immediately bolted off the stage, leaving the musical director with his baton in the air waiting for "Come here! come here!" Our stage manager, Barker, a good-hearted but grim-mannered fellow, rushed up to George Power, who said plaintively, "It's no use, Barker, you must send on the understudy." Barker's reply was to grab him by the collar and literally hurl him on to the stage, exclaiming, "Idiot! d'you think I keep the under-studies in the wings on a leash?"

There was a wonderful performance of *Pinafore* given entirely by children, all of them taught by Barker, and it was beautiful to see how gentle this rough man could be and the pride he took in their efforts to please him. At the first perform-ance I was standing beside him in the wings when

the Middy bars the way to Josephine.   Imagine the
size of this Midshipman when all the others were
children.   The little mite did it splendidly, and
Barker exclaimed in a tone of delight, "Bless his
little heart.   I knew he'd do it, damn him!"   I do
not know what became of the majority of these
clever children, but the juvenile lover made a certain
success later as Henry Eversfield.

Among the many charming people associated with
us at this time, there was no more genial and delightful personality than that of our musical director,
dear, sweet-natured Alfred Cellier, the composer of
many charming songs, some of which will live while
music lives.   He was also one of Sullivan's two
closest friends, the other one being Frederic Clay,
the same type of man and also a composer of note,
as evidenced by the undying and deserved popularity
of one song above all others, "I'll sing thee songs
of Araby"   To me, standing practically on the
threshold of a new kind of existence, it was a source
of intense gratification and delight to be treated *en
camarade* by these two men, so distinguished in the
world of art and so popular in that of Bohemia; and
a Bohemia that I venture to think does not exist in
these latter days, owing not only to the changed
conditions, but also to the necessarily unwieldy pro-
portions it assumes.

The only drawback to much association with
Alfred Cellier lay in the somewhat upsetting manner
he had of turning night into day, seldom putting in

an appearance before lunch-time, and being abnormally wide awake when some of us were longing for bed. But in this respect he was no worse than another well-known man whom I was proud to call my friend, E. L. Blanchard (the "old boy" of so many Drury Lane pantomimes), to walk and talk with whom was an education, the lesson frequently ending at a most fascinating little club called the Arundel, which, if I remember rightly, only opened its hospitable doors at midnight, and where there was always a kettle of boiling water for hot grog on a tripod on the centre table in the room. I am not sure what time the club closed, but I have several times left it and gone straight home to breakfast; and there were no such things as fines in those days, such as are inflicted now if one stays in the club after three.

Apart from the licensed critic, many people used to say of me that it was little wonder I played the vicar well, as my father was in the Church; and when it came to the turn of *Pinafore* they discovered an identical line of reasoning in that I had a brother in the Navy. No allowance was made, either for the possibility of lurking talent or the bringing out thereof by the ablest stage-manager I have ever seen at work—Gilbert, to wit—oh dear no! But this line of argument failed a little later when we produced *The Pirates of Penzance*, in which I played a Sergeant of Police, as in spite of all efforts they could not unearth for me a relative in the Force.

There was a flutter of excitement all round the theatre one night when we found that **H.R.H.** the Prince of Wales had announced his intention of coming. Our first Royal visitor, and, to add lustre to the occasion, Sullivan was to personally conduct the opera. We all looked forward to a brilliant and delightful evening, and I believe we had it; in fact, I am sure we did, with one exception—myself—and it was absolutely spoilt for me. Whether it was that in the course of so many performances we had altered the *tempo*, or that Sullivan after so long an absence had forgotten what it should have been, will never be known, but the fact remains that he took the Captain's first song so slowly that it not only missed the usual encore, but absolutely went without a hand. I could have cried—indeed, I believe I did— and I had a terrible feeling that His Royal Highness would never forgive me. Of the rest of the evening I remember nothing. How human nature measures everything by a personal foot-rule!

Another exciting evening during this run came when we were playing as a front piece a charming little one-act opera, by James Albery, called *The Spectre Knight*, with some of Alfred Cellier's most delightful music in it, notably two quartettes which live in my memory to this day, and which I should love to hear again. Richard Temple was the Knight, and was also the Dick Deadeye in *Pinafore*, and as my dear old friend was always suffering from a kind of contempt for anything less majestic than what is

SIR RUPERT MURGATROYD IN "RUDDIGORE." (ACT II.)

known as English Opera (which generally consists of
Italian Opera played in English, I fancy), he was
always giving odd performances of different operas,
in which he played the leading part.

He had arranged one of these for a Saturday night
at the Alexandra Palace, and I could not understand
how he meant to be in two places at once. However,
he murmured mysteriously that "it would be all right";
but it was not, for on the night in question came a
telegram from the Palace to say, " Unable find substitute, must remain here for Rigoletto." We had
to keep the curtain down for the first piece as no
one could wear the Knight's armour, and of course
the understudy had to go on for Deadeye.

We all thought Temple would suffer nothing less
than decapitation for this escapade, but he seems
none the worse for it to this day; but in spite of his
apparently escaping scot-free, I must admit that I
should never have dared such a thing on my own
account, and I feel sure he could not have given a
good rendering of Rigoletto with such a crime on
his mind. Temple was rather good-looking in those
days (he has not altered much, I believe), and his
make-up as Deadeye, one eye being blind, was exceedingly good. I remember a visitor to the dressing-room one night complimenting him on it, and
remarking that "he should not have known him, it
was quite a dead identity."

III

I THINK it must have been during the run of *Pinafore* that I began to acquire that method of acting without effort which has become, so I am told, one of my most marked characteristics. I have certainly found it a very valuable asset; for if there are many people who revel in bustle, there are as many, if not more, who prefer repose. However, it nearly proved fatal to my engagement, I believe, as when *The Pirates of Penzance* came to be cast I was told there was no part for me. Imagine my despair. With all the sanguine enthusiasm of youth and success, I had taken an elaborate set of chambers in some mansions just off the Strand, and furnished them comfortably, though not luxuriously, and the idea of being thrown out of employment raised the vision of an immediate sale of effects, followed by a lengthy sojourn in the workhouse. However, I heard that the part of the Sergeant of Police was not yet cast, and I so worked on the feelings of the powers that were that it was eventually given to me, and it turned out one of my greatest successes. It is an abnormally short part, being only on view seventeen minutes in all. I timed it one night, but

38

SERGEANT OF POLICE, IN "PIRATES OF PENZANCE."

into those seventeen minutes were crowded countless
opportunities of "scoring," of all of which I am
proud to remember Gilbert told me I took full
advantage.

We had a new *prima donna* for this piece—by the
way, in spite of our English tendencies (to which I
have already alluded), she was always called the
prima donna—who was a perfect picture to look at
and equally pleasant to listen to. This was Marion
Hood—tall, slight, and graceful, a typical English
girl with a wealth of fair hair which, I believe, was all
her own. Her singing of the waltz song, "Poor
Wandering One," was quite one of the features of the
first act, especially on account of what Sullivan himself called "the farmyard effects." I only appeared
in the second act, and my song, "The Enterprising
Burglar," was such an immense success that I had
always to repeat the last verse at least twice. It
occurred to me that an encore verse would be very
nice, and in a rash moment I one day presumed to
ask Gilbert to give me one. He informed me that
"encore" meant "sing it again." I never made such
a request again, but I heard it whispered that years
later, in a revival of the opera, the comedian playing
the part was allowed to sing the last verse in three
languages as an encore. The first performance of
Pirates very nearly had to be postponed on account
of an accident to Miss Everard, who was to have
played the part of Ruth; she was delightful as Little
Buttercup in *Pinafore.* She was standing in the

centre of the stage at rehearsal one morning, when I noticed the front piece of a stack of scenery falling forward. I called to her to run, and got my back against the falling wing and broke its force to a great extent, but it nevertheless caught her on the head, taking off a square of hair as neatly as if done with a razor. The shock and injury combined laid her up for some time, and there was consternation in view of a postponement. Fortunately I was able to suggest to Carte a clever and dear old friend of mine, by name Emily Cross, who I felt sure would be capable of replacing Miss Everard in the time. She was telegraphed for, and after much pressure she consented, and with only two days' study and rehearsal appeared and made a great success. She once told me a rather good little story against herself, of the days when she was a Shakespearean star-actress, and at the time playing Ariel at the Theatre Royal, Newcastle-on-Tyne, where she was a tremendous favourite. She was crossing Grey Street on a very wet and muddy morning, and being a careful woman raised her skirts well out of possible contact with the mud. Having crossed safely, she proceeded to lower them to the orthodox length, when a small street urchin remarked loudly, " Yow needn't be so particular about 'em, Emily ; we can see 'em *all* any night for tuppence."

The run of the *Pirates* marked two important crises in my life. I had always been a very keen footballer, and at this time was playing for the

Crystal Palace club, which, at its full strength, numbered some very good exponents of the game; indeed, when county football was inaugurated and the first match was played at the Oval between Surrey and Middlesex, I was one of five players on the one side fighting three on the other, all out of our first team—a pretty good average for one club. What jolly matches we had too all round London, even going as far as Chatham to play the Sappers (a long journey in those days), who then had Vidal and Marindin playing for them.

Forest School was one of our most enjoyable fixtures, and the scene of one of the crises I have alluded to, and also my last match. On arrival I found that I had not brought my barred boots with me; but, nothing daunted, I played in my walking boots, with the result that I came down heavily in turning, my right knee going out and in with two cracks like the report of a pistol. Of course, I "retired hurt," but after a spell of rest went, rather foolishly, to work again, with the same result. I got back to town in great pain, but went to the theatre as usual; but when I had been knocked down by the Pirate King and should have risen in my turn and felled him, I had to ask him to help me up. He kindly did so, and I went to bed for three weeks. No more football after that !

The other crisis was less exciting but equally mortifying in a way. Up to this time I had frequently been both honoured and flattered by receiving letters from anonymous correspondents breathing admiration and, in some instances, ardent passion. Some of them were, I know, genuine; how I know it this is neither the time nor place to explain, I may write a novel one of these days; but with the production of *Pirates* they ceased entirely. I incline to the belief that my appearance as the Policeman was regarded as being my true presentment, and they were therefore disillusioned. This point of view has subsequently been traversed by a cheerful doubt, induced by an intermittent recurrence of those charming attentions, up to within some ten years ago, when the force of circumstances compelled me in several plays to undertake the rôles of much-married foreign potentates, since which they have entirely ceased. Apropos this actor-worship, I was once at a ball where a lady to whom I had just been presented said, "Oh, Mr. Barrington, my daughter has fallen madly in love with you. May I introduce you ?" I murmured an embarrassed "Certainly," and she turned to a very pretty girl who was standing near, saying, "Marjorie, this is Mr. Rutland Barrington." The girl's face lit up with excitement and pleasure ; she took a good look at me, and turned away with a long and disappointed "Oh !" That mother knew something.

About this time the cult of æstheticism was invented, and it had some weird results, though it took such a firm hold on some people that to this day we see strong evidences of its transmission from mother to daughter, the highly æsthetic young man being fortunately about as extinct as the dodo.

To such a man as Gilbert the chance of shooting folly as it flew naturally proved irresistible, and the result was the writing of *Patience*, quite one of the most delightful operas of the series, which was produced at the Opera Comique in 1880. My part of the Idyllic Poet was originally christened Algernon Grosvenor, but was eventually changed to Archibald at the request of the rightful bearer of the original name, though I could never understand why such a notoriously athletic man and golfer as he was should have been nervous of unfavourable comparison.

Patience was a great success from the commencement, and Carte who had earlier begun to realize that a larger, more beautiful, and permanent home would be wanted for what appeared to be a class of entertainment that had come to stay, expedited the building of the Savoy Theatre with the intention of migrating there with our latest success. It was indeed an exciting evening in our lives when the move was made, and the welcome given to us in our new home was something to remember. At this lapse of time I am not quite certain whether there was a break in the performance or not, but I rather think we played one night at the Opera Comique and the next at the Savoy. I had another strong reason for remembering this first night, for I was almost voiceless. I had implored both Carte and Sullivan to excuse me from playing (my dialogue I could speak, so had no occasion to trouble Gilbert), but they declared they would rather have me with no voice than alter the cast on such an occasion. I was glad afterwards that they had been firm about it. After the Opera Comique both the stage and auditorium of our new home seemed enormous. There was one very excellent arrangement for the convenience of the artists in crossing from one side of the stage to the other (which was impossible at the Opera Comique without going underneath the stage) in the shape of a kind of recess at the extreme back of the stage, with an arched passage on either side. We were all pleased with this, but the scenic artist had noticed it also, and when the curtain rose on the first night we found the recess in use for the set and ropes put up to prevent any one crossing in sight of the audience, and we never had the use of that passage, but went under as before. Still, it was very sweet of the architect to design it specially for us. The passage and the arches have now totally vanished, under the order of the L.C.C. In addition to my voice trouble on the first night, I had another awful contretemps to contend with. When I took my seat on a rustic tree-trunk preparatory to singing "The Magnet and Churn," I heard an ominous kind of "r-r-r-i-p-p-p!" and immediately felt conscious of a horrible draught on my right leg. I knew, of course, what had happened; my beautiful velvet knee-

Photograph Elliott & Fry

ARCHIBALD GROSVENOR. IN "PATIENCE," SINGING "THE MAGNET
AND THE CHURN."

breeches had gone crack. It was an awful moment, as I could not possibly ascertain the extent of the damage, and had a song to sing and a scene to play before I could leave the stage. Had they but been made of red velvet it would not have mattered so much, for I felt I was blushing all over and it might have escaped notice, though some of the æsthetic maidens were already choking with laughter. What I did was, to shuffle all through the scene, and shuffle off sideways as soon as I could; but no one who has not suffered a similar experience can guess at the agony of mind I went through.

One night Richard Temple, who was playing Strephon, failed to appear at one of his entrances, when he should have rushed on singing "'Tis I, young Strephon." We waited for what seemed like half an hour, amid the noise of scuffling feet and shouts of "Temple! Mr. Temple!" in the wings, but there was no sign of him. I then sauntered off the stage, endeavouring to give the impression that I was going nowhere in particular, and the moment I was out of sight rushed to the green-room, where I found him half asleep over a newspaper. I dragged him to the stage, gave him his note, and (being an old hand at the game) he went on quite calmly and picked up his cue, and behold! he was one-sixteenth *sharp*. It was a score for me.

In 1882 *Patience* was followed by *Iolanthe*, which, by the way, was originally christened *Perola*, a kind of superstition having arisen in favour of titles beginning with a " P," and why it was changed I do not remember, but certainly *Iolanthe* is the prettier. It was in this play that one of the less important but beautiful fairies captivated the attention of a certain young peer who afterwards proved fickle, at considerable cost to himself. He mystified me very much one night when visiting my dressing-room, before I was aware of the attachment which made him such a frequent caller on Grossmith or myself, by saying, on my remarking that he would shortly know the piece by heart, " Well, is not she worth it?" It puzzled me for days—in fact, until the engagement was announced.

Durward Lely and I had a scene to play, as Tolloller and Mount Ararat, which, at rehearsal, appealed to both of us as so intensely funny that we absolutely could not get on with it for laughing, this occurring for several days running, until we were almost hysterical over it. Gilbert said he only hoped the audience would laugh half as much as we did, but on the first night they did not. I believe we both funked it, and consequently did not play it well, because it was afterwards quite one of the best scenes in the piece; but our blank looks on the first performance must have been funny.

Somewhere about this time a " curtain-raiser " called *The Carp* was produced, in which I, as an angler, was much interested. The angler was played by Eric Lewis, who had lately taken to the stage after a preliminary canter over the entertainment course, much the same as Grossmith and myself. At the end of the play each night he caught the fish, and was very triumphant over it; and being a pretty little piece, and clever, it ran for a long time— in fact, so long, that one night on the capture of the carp, a voice from the gallery came, in answer to Eric Lewis's joyful " I've caught it ! " with, " About time, too; it's high by now ! "

My old friend Arthur Law, who was then a bud- ding author, was another recruit to our ranks during this piece, being engaged to understudy me as Archi- bald Grosvenor. Before finally committing himself to the engagement, he paid me the compliment of asking my advice on the contract he was expected to sign. It was certainly one of the most comprehen- sive documents I ever read, as after the usual clauses to the effect that he was to " understudy, play old men, women, or juveniles, and anything he might be cast for," it ended with this highly humorous clause, " and write first pieces when required "; and all this on a weekly salary, and " weekly " might well have been spelt with an " a."

Iolanthe was the medium of Rosina Brandram's first great success. Jessie Bond was ill, and she was the understudy, and I well remember how she electri- fied the house with her glorious singing of the song in the second act where she appeals to the Lord Chancellor for her son. I have never heard a con- tralto singer who gave me so much pleasure as Rosina; she sang without any effort, and her voice had a fullness and mellifluous quality which were unrivalled. She did not shine as an actress, and I frequently expressed my surprise that she did not turn her attention to Oratorio; she always said she would like to, but I think the glamour of the stage life was too strong for her.

Iolanthe also furnished the debut of Manners, who was the original sentry and scored a great success with his song. This is yet another instance of the success of a part not being influenced by its length, as it is, if anything, shorter than the Sergeant of Police in *Pirates*, but presented equal opportunities of scoring. I wonder whether in all the parts he now plays, or has played, with the Moody Manners Opera Company he has found one which brought as much kudos with as little effort.

Here is a quaint little series of coincidences in connection with *Iolanthe*. I was writing a part of this chapter, dealing with the piece, while on a visit to Worthing, where I was giving a recital, and on finishing my morning's work went to pay a call on the local entrepreneur, who also edits and runs the local newspaper. He had just got out his "contents" bill, and the headline was "Iolanthe"; it referred to a school performance in the neighbourhood. While we were chatting the town band took up a position opposite us, and, of all things, started playing an *Iolanthe* selection, beginning with my song. To complete the humour of the situation,

Pho'ograph Elliott & Fry

LORD MOUNT ARARAT, IN "IOLANTHE"

when I turned to my friend and asked him what the air was, he failed to recognize it.

Alice Barnett, the original Fairy Queen, had a voice which was almost as massive as herself, and I remember how pleased she was with the shout of laughter which greeted her allusion to Captain Shaw in her apostrophe to Love. All the heads in the house turned to the stall which was occupied by the gallant fireman, the mention of whose name called forth a round of applause. There was something almost pathetic in the recollection to many of those present in 1907 at the revival of the opera, for although the veteran was present, time and illness had robbed him to a great extent of the old erect and gallant bearing.

IV

THOSE of us at the Savoy who had seen and heard the original cast of *Trial by Jury* were excited and pleased when the news came that it was to be played there.

I have to this day a vivid recollection of Arthur Sullivan's brother Fred as the original creator of the Learned Judge, and a most excellent performance he gave, full of that restrained humour which is imperative in dealing with Gilbert's work, a point which so many comedians fail to realize. Nellie Bromley was the Plaintiff, and a very lovely one too, and Walter Fisher the Defendant. He had a charming and sympathetic voice, and was one of the very few tenors it has been my good fortune to meet who could act as well as sing. This was the first piece in which Gilbert and Sullivan collaborated, and it possesses a perennial gaiety and freshness which is not eclipsed by any of its successors. I forget who was the original Counsel for the Plaintiff, but at the Savoy the part was handed to me, and I remember it as a very hard-working one, without, in my humble opinion, much opportunity. At a later

Photograph : The London Stereoscopic Company.

CORCORAN, A.B , "H M S. PINAFORE." (ORIGINAL PRODUCTION)

production of the Cantata I was cast for the Judge, and was happy to find that I had pleased Gilbert with my rendering, though I honestly think the Judge rather resembles Hamlet, in that it is so good a part that no one could absolutely fail in it. However this may be, I fancy no one but myself has played it since, and I seem to have established a kind of pre-scriptive right to the part. I consider myself extra fortunate in this because *Trial by Jury* is played at nearly all the big benefits and testimonial perform-ances, owing to the facility for introducing a crowd of well-known people who can "appear" in Court, thus not only assisting the cause without the dubious pleasure of rehearsing, but also bringing the pleasure of meeting many friends, colleagues, and acquaintances whom one otherwise would never see.

For instance, at the Ellen Terry Testimonial I had on the Bench beside me, among other stars, Mrs. Bernard Beere, Miss Lottie Venne, and Miss Geneviève Ward, while in the well of the Court was Lady Bancroft, so interested in the vagaries of the Judge that she stood up during the whole of the performance and fixed me with her lorgnettes. Among the Jury were Fred Terry, Cecil Raleigh, Anthony Hope, Arthur Collins, Martin Harvey, and many more, and they had an excellent Foreman in the person of Captain Robert Marshall; but as he had not appeared in opera for some time (so he told me), he was so occupied in watching the beat that it somewhat detracted from the humour of his performance. At any rate, this was his excuse for eventually missing his cue; but I have a notion that it was really caused by his strict attention to the "business" of the part, which consists in solacing the Plaintiff with his attentions, a task which all his fellow-jurymen seemed to envy him—and no wonder, for the Plaintiff was Ruth Vincent.

I remember upsetting the "crowd in court" at the Savoy very much one night (luckily, Gilbert was not present) in this way. On the left hand of the Bench the scene was painted to represent a bookcase filled with legal volumes, and at one part of the piece I rose from my seat, went to the side, and appeared to be looking for a book of reference. This, of course, was all in order, but when I proceeded to take a large book out of the painted canvas wonderment gave way in a moment to laughter; of course I had secreted it under my robe. I have been associated with many different Plaintiffs, all of them very pretty girls, but what concerned me more than their looks was how much they weighed. At the final picture, when cupids with garlands of roses descend and red fire is lighted, it is customary for the Learned Judge, as the central figure, to support the Plaintiff à la Harlequin and Columbine, she placing one dainty foot in his hands, which are held behind his back as he kneels, and then balancing herself with the knee pressing against his shoulders. It is not an easy task with a fairylike Plaintiff, and with some of the more robust type it has proved a trial of

THE LEARNED JUDGE, IN "TRIAL BY JURY."

strength and afforded an anxious moment. The bevy of bridesmaids also affords great scope for the inclusion of young and pretty actresses, and on these special occasions is invariably headed by Phyllis Broughton, to whom I have, in my official capacity, sent many little notes of admiration through the medium of my Usher.

The Usher is one of the funniest parts ever written, but as he is so seldom played seriously the spectator is hardly aware of this. On one occasion the comedian who was playing the part introduced some business of his own invention, if you please. Gilbert, who was not present, heard of it, and when writing to me, explaining why he had not been able to come, alluded to it, and said, "God bless him for it!" Marius and Courtice Pounds have been the best Defendants I have seen, and Eric Lewis and Hayden Coffin the two best Counsel, but even the personal popularity of the two latter failed to make the part stand out, in spite of the excellent song it contains.

Princess Ida was our next production, and to my mind the second act of this opera provided a veritable feast of music never excelled in any of the series. I did not appear in this act at all, and frequently used to stand in the wings to listen to it. I see that since writing this my opinion has been endorsed in print by George Grossmith and Workman.

I always considered my part of King Hildebrand in this opera the poorest which I had to play in all the series, and I was confirmed in my idea by the fact of Gilbert consenting to my wearing a beard for it—an adornment he usually objected to on the ground that he thought it, to a great extent, masked the expression of the face. Being such a very conscientious artist, I went the length of growing my own beard for the part. It was also a great saving of trouble and spirit-gum, but on receiving the proof of a photograph I had taken of myself, I went off hurriedly to Shipwright's and had it removed. I have never seen it since.

This production was notable for an innovation, being the first opera we had played in three acts, but I fancy it was not altogether a successful one; it certainly was not reverted to in future. The fact that it did not achieve a very long run I attributed very largely to King Hildebrand not being sufficiently prominent, and I well remember telling Carte as much and his agreeing with me—a condition of affairs that I should somehow have taken advantage of, but which I failed to do.

I made my bow as an author during the run of this piece, Carte most kindly allowing me the use of the Savoy for a matinée of an original play of my own which I called *Bartonmere Towers*. Amongst others who played in it were Cyril Maude, Frank Lacy, Yorke Stephens, Philip Cunningham, and Lily Hanbury, Yorke Stephens giving a very excellent performance of the villain. Some of the criticisms were quite favourable, but one I remember best expressed a doubt as to whether I had written a

Photograph   Elliott & Fry

KING HILDEBRAND IN "PRINCESS IDA."

comedy or a farce. I knew which it was—it was neither the one nor the other, but a comedy-drama.

Now was to come the most wonderful of all the series of these operas, the *Mikado*. There was not anything approaching our present knowledge of Japan and the Japanese existing at that time, and the mere presence of a small collection of people at Knightsbridge, under the name of "The Japanese Village," was creating quite a stir. Consequently the news that the next Savoy opera would be Japanese whetted public curiosity, and many were the efforts made to "tap" members of the company, and even choristers, for information. Of course, it was one of our unwritten laws that no particulars acquired at rehearsal were to be given to any one outside the theatre, and this was wonderfully well maintained; in fact, I believe the law was only broken once, and the offender was never discovered, or I feel sure he would have had "something with boiling oil in it."

Never during the whole of my experience have I assisted at such an enthusiastic first night as greeted this delightful work. From the moment the curtain rose on the Court swells in Japanese plate attitudes to its final fall it was one long succession of up-roarious laughter at the libretto and overwhelming applause for the music. On making my first en-trance I was rather disappointed to miss the usual "reception"; however, it came when I had spoken my first line, together with a roar of laughter, and I then realized that my make-up had rendered me for the moment unrecognizable. The trio and chorus, "Three Little Maids from School," sung by Leonora Braham, Jessie Bond, and Sybil Grey, was received with such enthusiasm and insistent encores as no musical number in my experience, or I believe any one's else, has ever equalled. It seemed as if we should never get on with the piece. Later on in the run its glories faded a little before the elaborated business of "The Flowers of Spring," which on the first night bloomed more soberly, although quite a feature.

One of the most enjoyable functions connected with the rehearsal of a new opera was the call for "music only" for the principal artists at Sullivan's flat in Victoria Street, where we would assemble and hear at first hand our songs, duets, and concerted numbers, and our interest was naturally intense and immense. I arrived at one of these calls (for *Mikado*) before my time on one occasion, being a very punctual man, punctuality not being looked upon as a virtue at the Savoy but as a matter of course, to find poor Sullivan looking an absolute wreck. He was a terrible sufferer from ill-health, and he told me he had passed a fearful night, and at four o'clock could not rest in bed, so had risen and walked about from room to room thinking over the composition of a song. "Just listen to this, B.," he said, and sat down to the piano and sang me one of the daintiest gems he has ever written, Yum-Yum's song, "The Moon and I " What man or woman listening to it could ever dream that it was written under such stress of pain as he described?

During rehearsals it was evident to me that Gilbert was not quite satisfied with my rendering of Pooh Bah, and it worried me considerably, because I could not quite make out what he wanted. I naturally tried my hardest to fall in with his wishes, and things seemed a little better, but when I said to him after some fortnight's work, "I hope that is more what you want," his reply came as rather a shock, "My dear Barrington, I have no doubt it will be an admirable performance, but it is no more my idea of Pooh Bah than chalk is like cheese." I then suggested that possibly a quiet visit paid to him at home, coupled with an hour or two's devotion to the exposition of his views might have the desired effect. This was duly carried out, and as Gilbert afterwards said, the upshot was a performance that exactly embodied his idea of the part. My recompense came at the end of the first performance, when he came to my dressing-room (this was a record also) and thanked me for "my invaluable aid to the success of the piece."

Richard Temple was our Mikado, and I do not think any one could wish for a better; but he used to get very angry at times with Grossmith, Jessie Bond, and myself for rolling about the stage in an excess of agony when he sentenced us to death. He declared it was not "art," and there is not much doubt that he was right, but the audience thoroughly enjoyed our antics, and the squeezing and slapping poor Jessie Bond received at our hands. She was continually threatening to complain about it to Gilbert, and I cannot think why she never did. There was another practical joke of mine that she pretended caused her a deal of annoyance, thus: driving up one night in a hansom to the stage door just as she was going in, some spirit of mischief prompted me to borrow four shillings of her for my fare, and this I paid back in numerous instalments, all of which were tendered on the stage during our scenes together (of course, quite unseen by the audience), and accepted angrily. Sometimes I would hand her a stamp, a penny, or two or three halfpence, with strict instructions that she should keep an account of what she received. She always declared that she never got her four shillings, but I believe my fun cost me at least six, and even then was cheap.

Temple had a narrow escape of losing his song, " My Object all Sublime," as for some reason Gilbert decided at the dress rehearsal that it would not go, and had better be cut. Cut it was, there and then, much to Temple's chagrin ; but when the choristers heard the news they went in a body to Gilbert and implored him to reinstate it. This was done, with what success we know.

This must have been an anxious first night for Gilbert, as, in addition to being a little worried about me, he was in the same state of mind about Grossmith, who also had not been shaping quite as he wished at rehearsals; indeed, George's performance on the production was nothing like so good as it became very shortly afterwards. I fancy the costume hampered him somewhat.

The value of Rosina Brandram's glorious voice in these operas was almost incalculable; it takes a singer of more than ordinary ability to arrest the attention of an audience and make a success even with such a delightful little song as "Hearts do not Break," when it comes without a word of dialogue immediately upon the uproarious fun of such a number as "The Flowers of Spring," but she accomplished the task.

Durward Lely was a capital Nanki Poo; indeed, to my mind, by far the best we have had, the part being a very manly one for a tenor, as distinct from the usual romantic type of hero.

To follow such a phenomenal success as *Mikado* was bound to be a difficult matter, and must have cost Gilbert many anxious and thoughtful moments. However, it had to be followed by something, and 1887 saw the production of *Ruddigore*. There is no getting away from the fact that it was, for the Savoy, a very stormy first night, some of the malcontents in the gallery shouting "Take it away—give us back the *Mikado*"; in spite of which, however, it achieved a run of some twelve months, a thing that many modern managers would consider quite good enough; but it so impressed me as a kind of failure that I once alluded to it as such in conversation with

Gilbert, who remarked, "I could do with a few more such failures," which I quite understood when he proceeded to mention the amount of his share of the profits on it. Still, the fact remains that it was responsible for what had been hitherto an unheard-of occurrence with us, a rehearsal the morning after the production, for cuts. Opinions would appear to be very conflicting about the opera, as more people have of late years expressed to me their surprise at its non-revival than of that of any other piece. Perhaps my point of view of the opera took on a jaundiced complexion, owing to the fact that during the rehearsals for it occurred what I may call my only serious disagreement with Gilbert, which happened thus ·

Certain people had been in the habit of asking him to allow them to be present at a rehearsal, and as he could see no objection, certain people were present at odd times ; but it got on the nerves of the artists engaged to a very great extent (artists are always touchy about things), and they resented —silently, be it said—being practically taught their business before strangers.

We held a consultation, and I proposed that a deputation should wait on Gilbert and ask him "not to do it again." This was voted a capital idea, but nobody would assist on the deputation, so Carte was invited to approach the great man on the subject. He sternly refused to interfere in any way, so matters were at a deadlock.

On one eventful morning, however, I suppose I must have had a liver attack or something (the only way I can account for going about the matter the wrong way), and I declined to rehearse "before a row of stalls filled with strangers." Then the breezes blew! Gilbert was, very naturally, very angry, and, also very naturally, did not omit to say so; but matters were eventually adjusted, and all was peace once more. I find on referring to the letters which passed between Gilbert and myself on the subject, that I personally knew all the people who were present. Professor Herkomer and Frank Burnand were two of them, the former having expressed a special desire to attend an "early" rehearsal so that he might observe Gilbert's method, the fact being that just then he was giving a performance of some play in his studio at Bushey, and hoped to pick up a useful hint or two. I was invited later to see the play, in which he made great experiments with a harvest moon, I believe, but I was unable to go.

Although Gilbert quite forgave me my little outburst, he nevertheless for some days after "rubbed it in" by saying to any of the company who were watching from the stalls while awaiting their next cue, "You mustn't sit here, Barrington won't like it"; but after all our object was attained and we rehearsed in comfort, so I did not mind being a scapegoat in a small way, more especially as I knew that the rubbing in was done in a spirit of fun, for once a disagreement was settled, Gilbert was never the man to bear malice.

In support of my argument of how trying such an experience might be to an artist, there was a member of the company with one line to speak, "It's like eight hours at the seaside," and, try as he would, he could not catch the inflection Gilbert wanted; he made it about sixteen, and I know it took quite eight to get it anywhere near right, and the whole company felt on thorns whenever this speech was approached at rehearsal.

There was a very pretty girl engaged for a minor part in one of these operas, and at her first rehearsal she spoke her lines with a most fascinating French accent, not knowing, evidently, that we were nothing if not English. Gilbert at once stopped her. "Excuse me, but is that your usual mode of speech?" "Yes," was the reply; "it is a paarrt of me, and I think it ees varree naice." "Possibly," said Gilbert, "but, you see, we are an English company, so I am afraid——" He was interrupted by the lady saying with a strong Cockney twang, "Well, I can drop it if I like."

V

GILBERT—SULLIVAN—CARTE

Apart from my business associations, it was my
privilege to see something of all the great Triumvirate, as they have been called, in their private life,
though a great deal less of Sullivan than of the other
two. I have had the pleasure of being a guest in the
houses of all, and could not wish for better hosts,
albeit so dissimilar in tastes and pursuits.

With Gilbert there was always a certain feeling
which I can only describe as a sensation of living in
a kind of mental firework factory. But, mind you,
Brock's best all the time; none of your common
squibs and crackers, and he seemed to keep the fuse
alight all the time without the slightest effort.

Though invariably anxious for each guest to amuse
himself or herself as they might desire, he was
always ready to join in any game that was going, and
occasionally inclined to be the least bit dictatorial on
the points connected with it, as, for instance, George
Grossmith and I found on one summer day when we
were staying with him near Uxbridge, and proposed
a sett of lawn tennis.

We discovered to our amazement that the court
was considerably longer than the regulation ones we

were used to. It appeared that Gilbert was a very hard hitter, and found it difficult to keep the ball within the court as laid down by the laws, and being a law to himself he extended the court. This sounds as humorous as one of Pooh Bah's speeches in *Mikado*, but is true.

His marvellous readiness undoubtedly did much to add to the effect of his witty sayings, and in all the years I have known him I do not recollect seeing him at a loss.

I trust that if he by any chance reads these lines he will not be annoyed at the past tense I am obliged to use, for it is true enough that at our last meeting no one was more present than he, and as quick as ever with the retort courteous.

On one occasion, when rehearsing *Pinafore*, he said, "Cross left on that speech, I think, Barrington, and sit on the skylight over the saloon pensively." I did so, but the stage carpenter had only sewn the thing together with packthread, and when I sat on it it collapsed entirely, whereupon he said like lightning, "That's *ex*pensively!"

Here is a story about Gilbert that I got at second hand, but which I have no reason to discredit on that account. When in New York he one night attended a soirée where he met a lady who professed a great interest in music, and after the usual compliments on Gilbert and Sullivan, she proceeded to discuss other composers, and remarked, "I do so admire Mr. Bach's music"—(she pronounced it Bayche). "Can you tell

Photograph   *Alfred Ellis & Walery*

SIR WILLIAM S GILBERT.

me if he is now composing?" "No, madam," said Gilbert, "he is decomposing."

I wish some one would prevail upon him to give his impressions of America and Americans. They would form very interesting reading, I feel sure.

Sullivan was somewhat of a *bon viveur* whenever he could escape the grip of his chronic malady, but was also most emphatically a gourmet, and invariably had an excellent *chef* in his employ. Gilbert, calling there one morning, was chaffing him about this, and Sullivan defended it by insisting that even the most simple dishes sounded more attractive in French. "For instance," said he, "look at my menu there for breakfast, and you will see what I mean." Gilbert picked it up and said, "Quite so. I see. Bloaters!"

That Sullivan was also a humorist is amply evidenced in his compositions, and naturally most strongly in his manipulation of the low comedian of the orchestra, the bassoon.

There was a *Pinafore* selection played at Covent Garden Promenade Concerts, and Sullivan was conducting a rehearsal. On arriving at the "What, never? Well, hardly ever!" of the Captain's song there was a silence. The bassoon player remarked, "There is a cadenza marked in my part, Mr. Sullivan, but it's not written." Sullivan explained the situation to him, and said, "Just ask yourself questions on the instrument, and answer them." The player did so, and every one present was convulsed with the quaint effect.

E

Apropos this instrument, there was invariably enormous competition for seats at the Savoy *premières,* and it was difficult to find room for all friends.   On one occasion a great personal friend of Sullivan's, Mr. Reuben Sassoon, had applied too late, and backed his application with a piteous appeal to Sullivan for help.   He at once said to Carte, " If he'll change the first letter of his name, I'll give him a seat in the orchestra."

The parties which Sullivan gave in his flat in Victoria Street were always eagerly looked forward to by. any of us lucky enough to be invited.   In addition to the honour of meeting Royalty, one had the great pleasure of hearing the *crème de la crème* of every branch of talent then before the public, for each and all were pleased with an opportunity to do ever so slight a service to the man whose geniality won all hearts.   I have heard in his drawing-room Albani singing with Sullivan as accompanist, and the Duke of Edinburgh playing a violin obbligato, to be followed by the latest and most chic of speciality artists, and then some trio or song from the piece then running at the Savoy.   Santley, Edward Lloyd, Norman Salmond, Hollman, Antoinette Sterling, Arthur Roberts, Albani, Trebelli, Jessie Bond, to mention only a few of the names of people I have seen there on one evening, will give some idea of the excellence and variety of the entertainment.

When our music was handed out at rehearsal it consisted only of what is known as a " voice part," and we were expected to read it at least fairly well at sight. I was always very brave at this business, and no fence was too stiff for me to tackle, in spite of an occasional severe fall. When this happened, Sullivan would smile his sweetest and say : " Very good tune indeed, B.; now we'll have mine." As a matter of fact, he would deliberately lay little traps for me, and I remember one, of a sudden change of time, which, for a wonder, failed to catch me, to my intense delight, greatly added to by Sullivan's whimsical expression of astonishment and disappointment. He was most kind in altering songs for us if we desired, which did not often happen; but one of my treasures is part of a song so altered for me and signed by him.

One of the most delightful weeks of my life was spent as his guest at Roquebrune, where he used to take a villa for the winter. I had written a two-act opera which I was very anxious to submit for his consideration, with a view to production at the Savoy in the event of his not again collaborating with Gilbert, which at this time was just possible, and he kindly suggested that I should take a week's holiday with him and bring the play. After hearing it he expressed his satisfaction, and was most complimentary about my lyrics, and his last words were a provisional promise to set my book; but, as every one knows, matters were adjusted between the partners, and my piece went into the retirement shared by a good few others I have written.

I shall never forget that, my first and last visit to the South of France and Monte Carlo. I travelled from London to Paris with Walter Austin, the well-known professor of music, and robbed him shamefully at piquet, I remember; but from there I went on alone, at which I was very pleased, as I was feeling like a boy out for a holiday, and wanted to give the feeling full play.

After a modest dinner I left Paris by the night train, but sleep was the last thing I thought of. Wherever we stopped I got out to have a look round, and had several narrow squeaks of being left behind, most particularly at some station just about as day was breaking, when I was attracted by the sight of a long table on the platform bearing cups of steaming hot coffee and rolls. I was only about half through my refreshment when the official made the usual announcement about getting in again. I collected my best French and said, "Attendez, s'il vous plait; je n'ai pas fini mon café." The French gentleman rolled off a long and evidently indignant sentence. I said, "Plait-il?" He replied very angrily, "Le train va partir," to which I answered in my best declamatory style, and with arm extended in a commanding manner, "Le train ne peut partir sans moi!" Fortunately for me, it seemed to take away his breath for a minute or so, and I finished my breakfast. He then stalked off muttering something that sounded like "Un sacré milord anglais"; finally he blew a kind of penny trumpet, I jumped in, and

Photograph Chancellor

SIR ARTHUR SULLIVAN.

we were off; and I quite felt that I had asserted my nationality.

We used to go in to the Casino after lunch, and come out again to Roquebrune about six o'clock, so that we did not deprive ourselves of too much fresh air; but I am quite sure that if I ever stay in Monte itself, I shall find the attraction of the tables too strong for me. Sullivan always played the same coup; I do not know precisely what it was, but it was intimately connected with No. 11, round and on which he spread his louis. He had a bad day on the Wednesday, and on the following day declared his intention of not going in. However, I did not like leaving him alone, and also had a strong presentiment that his number would turn up, so he allowed himself to be persuaded, and to my great relief won a very considerable sum. There was another notable recollection connected with this visit. Sir Frederick Johnstone had asked Sullivan to dinner at his villa one night, and hearing that he had a visitor insisted on my being brought along, and to my great pleasure I sat next to Lord Randolph Churchill, whom I had never met before. He proved to be in great form, and I played the part of listener with great delight.

My last day at the tables was a variegated one. I had been doing moderately well. I may say I had only been playing five-franc pieces all the week, and when our usual time for train-catching arrived I was a winner. Sullivan, at the same table, had been having a bad run, which had just turned in his favour, so he proposed staying for six more coups and driving home. I thought six coups in gold could not hurt, but we eventually stayed an hour, and I wished we had gone home at our usual time; but my regret was tempered with the pleasure of another good win for my genial host, and my last evening was quite a success.

I crossed from Calais on Christmas Eve, and was absolutely the only passenger in the train to London. There were very few on the boat, and a thick fog nearly prevented our getting into Dover at all; but after leaving the ship it was plain sailing, and I got home to my Christmas dinner, and the table decoration was a branch of oranges picked by me in the open two days before.

Sullivan suggested one morning that I might like to lunch in Italy, and as this sounded rather novel and humorous I agreed. Accordingly we entrained for Ventimiglia, but the lunch was not a great success, and I sincerely trust there are Italian towns considerably less malodorous than this.

Very many happy days have I to ascribe to the geniality and hospitality of D'Oyly Carte, who was never happier than when surrounded by friends. He had a great fondness for all kinds of games, though unfortunately not possessed of the qualifications necessary to shine at any athletic pursuit, probably owing to want of opportunities when a boy. He had a great command of language, but it was almost invariably used on himself, with the most ludicrous effect. He had a quaint habit, for instance, when playing any kind of game and failing at a shot or stroke, of calling himself the most opprobrious names. I persuaded him to take up golf, and though he would never have made a player, he was most keen about it, and that was a game which afforded him limitless opportunities for indulging his odd characteristic. I was often quite unable to play on for laughing.

He was quite the most kind-hearted friend one could desire, and yet at the same time one of the hardest managers to deal with. When he started at the Opera Comique he had a Board of Directors, but before we went to the Savoy he had relieved himself of this incubus, and from what I have in later years learnt of boards and their ways, this one fact proves him a discerning man.

He was a considerate and tolerant employer, and his numberless kind actions to less fortunate people than himself should have secured him a fine record in the "Domesday Book." He shared the well-known weakness of other great men for sending telegrams, and when going anywhere by train, he was no sooner settled in his seat than he would ask for or produce a number of forms which he would fill up with no possibility of sending for ever so long a time.

He once asked me to go with him to Henley to give my opinion on a houseboat he thought of buying. Of course I was delighted to go, and asked him to include Grossmith in the party, with a view to some fun.

We started our day's amusement in the train by addressing Carte as " Pa " much to the delight of the other passengers, increased by D'Oyly's impatience under the imputation, culminating in his saying, "Shut up, you fools ! "

Our first joke matured at Shiplake, then a tiny little station, where we left the train and strolled on while Carte interviewed the stationmaster, and gave instructions concerning certain telegrams he expected to have found there and wished sent on to Henley. The way to the waterside lay through the meadows, and we had to pass through a gate which we carefully shut, and then waited for Carte. As he came up we yelled playfully, "Gate's locked, Pa, you've got to get over," and to our delight he believed us and clambered on to the top bar, by which time we had, of course, opened the gate and were gently swinging it to and fro. The remarks he made to us and the intentions he expressed were so forcible, that we had to bargain for immunity before letting him get down. For a short time we then displayed an exaggerated deference, which worried him a good deal ; but the climax of our fun was to come at lunch time. Carte, having ordered it, went to the station to inquire for telegrams, and as George and I both felt that he ought not to be disappointed of a message, we went quietly to the post office and sent one off to Shiplake station, to be sent on. It arrived during lunch, and it was worth all our trouble to hear D'Oyly's pleased "At last ! " The messenger claimed

Photograph   Alfred Ellis & Walery

RICHARD D'OYLY CARTE.

eighteenpence for porterage, which rather annoyed him, but he paid it, opened it, and read, " Come at once—baby much worse." For a moment he was completely puzzled, then he turned to us, and—we both went quietly but quickly out.

Carte was quite one of the best judges of a good cigar I ever knew, and yet, oddly enough, had an extraordinary predilection for smoking those of an inferior quality. He kept the very best for his friends, and always told you which was his own box, so that you knew which to avoid.

I persuaded him that there was a great opening for a really first-class hotel on one of the Thames islands somewhere near town, and he said if I would find the island he would think of it. I found it in due course ; he bought it, and began clearing it for building. We had some splendid times camping out on it in huts, but it was camping in comfort with professional cooking, and therefore really enjoyable.

When the hotel was finished the licence was opposed so vigorously by the local innkeepers that he at once relinquished the idea and converted it into a private house ; but for some time his guests were much puzzled over certain apparently eccentric arrangements, and he was several times asked why he had as many as twelve washhand basins on the ground floor. By degrees all signs of its original intention disappeared, and it became a most delightful place to stay in.

He once took the entire Savoy company for a trip

on the river in two launches, and we lunched in the lovely Clieveden woods. Coming home by moonlight we sang all the choruses and concerted music from the different operas, and the effect was perfectly delightful, drawing quite large houses at the different locks we passed through.

He was the first man to use electric light in a theatre, and came before the curtain on the first occasion to give a short lecture on its advantages.

He used periodically to come to me with a kind of veiled threat which he would endeavour, unsuccessfully, to deliver without a twinkle in his eye. It was this: "B., you must look out; there is a man in the provinces who plays your parts wonderfully, and *sings well.*"

His great kindness of heart caused him to keep in his service some very quaint persons in subordinate positions. One man was so hopelessly deaf, that whatever he might be told to do he simply went and poked the fire and resumed his seat; while another was inclined to be impertinent, and used to get his notice to leave "there and then" at least once a week, but he always turned up the next morning, and Carte either forgot or forgave—the latter most frequently, I believe.

This man appeared one day in great distress, and on being questioned announced that "his touring company was not doing well." When Carte had recovered from his astonishment, he asked what the company was. "*The Wobbling Wonders,*" was the reply. "There's six of 'em, and they was wobbling at Chatham last night to 4s. 6d. ! " But it seemed there was an additional cause of trouble in the fact that "his first wife had turned up." "How turned up?" said Carte. "I mean she's found me, and it's so unpleasant for my second." He did not seem to think it bad for himself, so noble-natured is man, but he had omitted to inform the second that he was already married. I never heard the sequel, but he was not long depressed.

One of the best excuses for dilatoriness I ever heard was made by a little old man who used to hang about the Savoy stage door on the look-out for odd jobs. I sent him one day to the post office just across the road for some stamps, and he was nearly an hour gone, and his change was short on his return. When I asked him the reason of his delay, he said, "I'm sorry, sir, but I had to wait while they made 'em."

Carte was most sympathetic and kind about my venture with management, an attitude which appealed to me very strongly in view of the fact that it was, so to speak, a kind of desertion from the banner under which I had made my first London success, and I am truly glad to say that we remained the firmest of friends until the day of his death, though we naturally saw little of each other in later years.

VI

ST. JAMES'S—"THE DEAN'S DAUGHTER"—"BRANTING-
HAM HALL"—COMEDY—"MERRY MARGATE"—
"PICKWICK"—"AREA BELLE"—SAVOY—"GONDO-
LIERS"

DURING the run of *Ruddigore* I developed a very
bad attack of ambition, which took the form of a
keen desire to be a manager of a theatre myself, and
the idea materialized when I received an offer of
substantial backing from a financier of my acquaintance. The St. James's was in the market, and I
secured a lease of it, having in view the production
of a comedy-drama entitled *The Dean's Daughter*,
by Sydney Grundy and F. C. Philips, the play being
a dramatization of a novel by the latter.

My self-elected financier proved, however, a broken
reed, and backed out of his promise after I had
signed the lease, leaving me with nothing but my
very modest savings to work with. I then obtained
an introduction to Colonel North, but for whose
kindness in stepping into the breach I should have
missed an experience which I cannot entirely regret,
though it brought me disaster.

I very much wanted my old friend Mrs. John
Wood to play a part in this piece, which she was

also inclined to do, and this would, I believe, have made an enormous difference in the result of my venture; but almost as she was on the point of signing with me, some people connected with the Court Theatre made her an offer that it would have been madness to refuse, and my hopes were dashed. She most kindly suggested that I should let my theatre and bring myself and the play to the Court, but it was impossible to arrange matters.

Olga Nethersole and Allan Aynesworth made their bows to London in this play, and I believe it might have been a commercial success but for one situation at the end of it. The unctuous hypocrisy of the Dean was a little too strong for the then state of mind of the theatre-goer—this was before the era of the so-called Problem Plays—but it was in vain that I begged of both authors to alter the end of the play, and let the meretricious cleric suffer and not the daughter he had practically sold for a deanery. In spite of this there could be no two opinions about the success of the piece on the first night, and this, too, in the face of what was an unpleasant and might have been a very awkward incident. About this time Clement Scott, who had established for himself a position which I fancy was unique in the annals of journalism, had said or done something to offend the patrons of pit and gallery, and on entering the stalls on the first night he received a decidedly hostile greeting, renewed after each act, and at the end of the evening becoming very stormy indeed, so much so that I ordered the lights to be turned down in the hope of clearing the theatre. I was greatly aided in obtaining the desired result by my old friend George Edwardes, who addressed the agitators somewhat to this effect: "Boys, you're not giving Barrington a fair chance. Go home quietly, and say what you like to Mr. Scott outside the theatre." This, I thought, was extremely friendly of George and very tactful, but he rather spoilt it with his peroration, "Don't forget the first night at the Gaiety next week."

D'Oyly Carte, who was present, came round to see me after the play, and when I expressed my uneasiness as to the financial side of the question, owing to the defection of my financier, consoled me with the remark, "Don't worry, B., you've got a success, and won't want any more money," thus giving one more instance of the uncertainty pertaining to all theatrical ventures; for though the piece went well enough with the people who came, they did not come in sufficient numbers, and I soon had to put its successor in rehearsal.

This was a drama called *Brantingham Hall*, written by W. S. Gilbert, being, in fact, the first play he had finished, without music, since his association with Sullivan.

In this play Julia Neilson made her first appearance on the stage, and it was also Lewis Waller's first London engagement, and the fact that they both scored very distinct successes, which they have since emphasized in many directions, as is also the case with Olga Nethersole and Allan Aynesworth, remains one of the few consoling items in this, to me, disastrous experience.

The critics found fault with the big situation of the play, in which the heroine, believing her husband dead and in order to save his father from ruin, declares that she never was his wife, but his mistress. They seemed to think—in fact, said—that no woman would go to such a length; and of course they may be right, but no one can say with any certainty what a woman will or will not do when greatly moved.

Whatever the cause, failure was the result, and a very unpleasant time for me the sequence. Gilbert very generously declined to accept any part of his author's fees; but other creditors were naturally unable to follow his lead, and eventually I emerged from the Bankruptcy Court free to make a fresh start.

My next appearance was at the Comedy Theatre, under the management of Charles Hawtrey, in a three-act farce by Sydney Grundy called *Merry Margate*, which was merry enough while it lasted, which was not long, and we followed this with a one-act piece by Burnand, founded on an episode in *Pickwick*, to which Edward Solomon had written some delightful music. Lottie Venne, Arthur Cecil, and myself represented Mrs. Bardell, Pickwick, and the Baker respectively. I am inclined to believe the baker to be an invention of Burnand's, as I do not remember any mention of him in *Pickwick;* but it was a good part, and the little piece used to go splendidly; indeed, I fancy it would reproduce well, as would also another one-act piece I played in by George Hawtrey, namely, *The Area Belle*, in which I played Tosser to the Pitcher of Dan Leno, for one occasion only.

I well remember Arthur Cecil's surprise and envy when we assembled at his chambers in the Haymarket for the first music rehearsal of *Pickwick*, and I read all mine off as if I knew it. He said it took him a week to learn one song.

He was notorious for his attention to detail in the parts he played, and we had an amusing instance of it in this piece, he suggesting some business with a butcher's account-book which Pickwick was to add up, but as it would have required at least four lines of dialogue to explain, it was cut.

He and Burnand eventually got so befogged over the stage management of the piece that they finally, on the suggestion of Solomon, handed over to me the task of production, and Arthur was so overjoyed at his respite that he presented me with a very quaint old Queen Anne punch-ladle, which I much prize. Another amusing incident in connection with *Pickwick* was the fact that, owing to some accident, the production was postponed at the very last moment, in spite of which a certain journal contained the next morning a violent diatribe against the piece and all concerned in it. It was possibly the only occasion on which I have been told I acted badly without deserving it, and then it may be only because I had not acted at all. Burnand, of course, brought an action, and was awarded damages. I was a witness, both disinterested and unpaid ; I think the first and last time I have been any of the three.

On one occasion we played *Pickwick* at the Crystal Palace at 7.30, having to get back to the Comedy in time to play it at 10.30. This was too much for Arthur Cecil, who went off to Brighton from the Palace, and I played *Pickwick* at the Comedy, Charlie Hawtrey himself playing the Baker ; but to my great chagrin he refused to take advantage of such a capital chance of giving his well-known imitation of me, and sang his music much less effectively in consequence.

Edward Solomon was a great loss to the musical comedy world, being absolutely brimming over with melodies that caught the ear at once—so essential to this type of entertainment ; and if not the highest form of composition, possessing at least a merit which at present appears somewhat lacking ; indeed, after mentioning Lionel Monckton and Ivan Caryll, one has to think for the next name.

He was also the best accompanist any one could desire, his work being an assistance to the singer instead of, as is so often the case, an effort to get the best of the battle. He once told me a story of himself against himself, which has one excellent moral, if possibly rather wanting in moral tone. He was in

F

New York and somewhat pressed for money, so took an old score to a manager and invited his attention to an opera "he had just written," played over two acts of it, not a note of which was there, sold it, and received a cheque on account.

So far so good, but, as he told me, he had one very anxious moment, for when he had quite finished the manager said, "Just play me that song for the soprano in the first act again, will you?" Of course he could hardly remember what he had played, but he dashed at it, and nothing was noticed. In justice to him I should say that the opera was eventually written and duly delivered. One striking peculiarity of his was that when composing it was almost necessary that there should be some one with him to keep up a constant conversation.

Shortly after these excursions into foreign parts, as it were, I returned to my old home for the production of *Gondoliers*.

That was a very memorable first night to me. For one thing, I was suffering from the kind of bruised-all-over feeling one gets after taking a heavy fall; and to this was added a nervousness as to my reception, for I felt very strongly that there was an atmosphere of sympathy for me about on account of the unfortunate result of my ambitious flight. Many people would say that this is just the kind of conceited idea an actor would have, but I still feel very proud of the justification realized by the warmth of my reception that night, and I also remember it as

GUISEPPE, IN "GONDOLIERS."

giving an opportunity to a brother artist to display a consideration and tact for which one might often look in vain.

Courtice Pounds and myself, as the two gondoliers, had to enter together in a boat, and we had hardly stepped out on to the stage and our greeting commenced, when he carefully hid behind some choristers until my welcome was ended. The public is always quick to recognize a graceful action, and his own reception was no less hearty on this account.

Shortly after this production Gilbert went off for a trip to Cairo, and on his return some one went to him with wild tales of gags introduced by me into the piece. This led to trouble, because as he would never see one of his own pieces from the front of the house, he had to accept the word of onlookers as to what was being done or left undone; and if, as was doubtless often the case, they held him and his work in such esteem as to consider a gag nothing less than profanation, one can understand the situation.

However, the mischief-makers were defeated on this occasion, as after some stormy correspondence and placid interviews, I prevailed with him to come and see the scenes complained of, which he did one night from the prompt entrance.

It was characteristic of him to leave the theatre without saying a word to me, and equally so that he should write me the pleasant note which lies among my treasures, to say: "Dear Barrington,—Everything admirable—alter nothing—go on and prosper."

The most memorable recollection in connection with *Gondoliers* is perhaps that of our visit to Windsor to play before Queen Victoria, the first theatrical company to obtain a " command " since the death of the Prince Consort.

What a state of excitement we were all in, to be sure! and how we promenaded the platform at Paddington, from which our "special" started, with an intense desire to tell every one where we were going, and what for!

D'Oyly had a harmless sort of mania for writing and sending telegrams, and Grossmith and I travelled down with him, and I don't think I ever saw so many forms filled up, except once, in an office in the Strand, where a tipster was sending off his selections.

I went with him to the office on our arrival at the Castle and sent off one on my own account to my wife, just " Have arrived," and both D'Oyly and myself were rather astonished to find there was nothing to pay; it was, of course, Her Majesty's private wire. I was more than glad afterwards that I had sent off my message as a kind of joke, because it happens to be the only souvenir of this memorable visit I have. There were no programmes issued, I believe.

We dressed in the large hall just off the Waterloo Chamber, where the stage had been fitted up, and having ascertained from one of the equerries that Her Majesty would pass close to the curtain behind which we were (indeed, we were told to keep very quiet during her passage), I quietly made a fair-sized hole in my curtain through which I had an excellent view of the Queen, whom I was most anxious to see at close quarters. I remember that Her Majesty enjoyed the performance immensely, beating time to many of the numbers, and laughing heartily at the fun of the piece and the humour of the dialogue.

We were a most uproarious crowd at supper, at which our party was augmented by several of the equerries and some of the invited guests who were personally known to Carte. I have no recollection of how we got back to town, but presume we did so, as the Savoy was open the next night and I got there in good time.

We all felt very proud of D'Oyly Carte, whom Her Majesty sent for and most graciously thanked, and we felt proportionately grateful because he gave himself no airs over the matter. I have met actors and actresses since, not to speak of managers, whose heads have been turned with far less excuse.

It was during my tenancy of the St. James's that I had the honour and pleasure of assisting at one of the dinner parties given to the dramatic profession by H.R.H. the Prince of Wales, our present King. This dinner took place on 12 March, 1893, and not the least memorable feature of the evening to me was that I sat next to G. A. Sala, whom I thus met for the first time. As he combined the solemnity of an epicure with the brilliance of one of the best of raconteurs, the intervals between the courses were only too short.

What a terrible percentage of my fellow-actors present at this dinner have joined the majority—Irving, Toole, David James, Terris, Farren, Arthur Cecil, and D'Oyly Carte.

THE VICAR OF BRAY. (ACT I.)

VII

ABOUT this time Sullivan began, I think, to tire ever
so little of his continuous devotion to comic opera,
and to sigh for a larger field of battle.   He must
also have affected Carte with the same idea, for while
he began to compose the music for *Ivanhoe*, for
which Sturgess provided the libretto, Carte began to
build what was intended to be a permanent home
for English Grand Opera, the result being one of
London's most beautiful theatres, which is now
known as The Palace Music Hall in Shaftesbury
Avenue.   How magnificently *Ivanhoe* was staged
and played!   There was a double company for the
opera, as it seems to be a tradition that Grand Opera
artists cannot possibly sing every night in the week.
I presume they are a more delicate race than the
hardy Comic Opera people.

Although *Ivanhoe* itself was a great success, the
venture was found impossible to work at anything
less than a heavy loss, and it ended with the final
dreadful transformation of the theatre into a music
hall.

I do not intend by this the slightest sneer at the

87

" Halls," in some of which, notably the Coliseum, I have been welcomed and made to feel happy ; but it did seem sad that this great attempt to found a home for English Opera, on the part of a successful manager and the greatest composer England has ever known, should meet with such a poor recompense.   And yet in the face of this failure there are periodical outcries for a National Theatre, which is not really desired.

In the meantime we had at the Savoy a fresh combination of talent in the persons of Sydney Grundy and Edward Solomon, who were responsible for *The Vicar of Bray*.   This opera, though lacking many of the most striking features of our former pieces, was a marvellous success, considering the standard that had been set up, and personally I simply revelled in the part of the Vicar—an extremely hard-working one, by the way, it being the nearest approach to a "one-part piece" I have ever played in.   So patent was this that one of the stage hands said to me one night, " Well, guv'nor, blest if you ain't carnin' all our money for us in this bloomin' piece ! " only he said neither " blest " nor " bloomin'."

By way of a kind of holiday, combined with business, I went on a short tour with *The Vicar* in the Isle of Wight, and as it was my first visit there I very much enjoyed it, although some of the places we played in were rather cramped, being for the most part town halls.   In Shanklin one night, just as I commenced my first song, a donkey outside

Photograph Alfred Ellis

THE VICAR OF BRAY. (ACT II.)

appeared to think he had also received his music cue, and as he was evidently the Lablache of his company the duel was manifestly unfair, and I eventually had to resign. I came forward and told the audience that I would continue my song as soon as my parishioner had finished. That put them in good humour; we waited a little in silence; the donkey finished with a cadenza in D major, and all was well. I was rather nervous of further interruptions, but he left the neighbourhood at the end of the first act, having, I think, discovered that in Act II I did a dance that he knew would be too much for him.

We had an awful experience on this tour in going from Jersey to Weymouth, where we were due to play about three hours after arrival. It was a terribly rough passage, the boat fairly standing on the rudder most of the time, and nearly every one was very ill. I was one of the lucky ones, but I nearly managed it when I went to the saloon for some dinner. We arrived safe and sound at Weymouth, but three hours late, so had to go direct to the theatre and begin. I do not know who was the architect of that theatre, but he could not have allowed for any foundations, for the whole place was going up and down like a ship at sea, and when it came to dancing I could not tell which foot was off the floor and which on, until I finally found that both were off, so sat down to reason it out. However, we worried through, and I was glad to seek the shelter of my hotel; but on the way there I met an old friend who was spending his holiday in Weymouth, and he was most enthusiastic about the fishing. Would I go with him? Certainly I would, but not then. "No; but will you come to-morrow?" I said I would think it over, as I had had nearly as much sea as I wanted. "Well," said he, "I shall call for you when I start." "All right," I answered; "at what time?" "About four," said he. "Very well," I replied, "but don't be vexed if I'm out." "Out, my dear fellow! You must have *some* sleep!" The lunatic meant four in the morning! I left hurriedly, and am glad to say I have never seen him since.

We returned to town in June, 1891, to give yet another author his chance at the Savoy, in the person of Mr. George Dance, whose *Nautch Girl* was, I believe, his maiden effort (no joke intended and none taken), and to this opera also Solomon set the music, and very charming indeed it was.

Solomon was one of my most loyal admirers, and I was much amused when he came to me one day in a great state of indignation because Dance had suggested that possibly the part of the Rajah of Chutneypore might be beyond my capabilities. The little man was honestly wroth at what he considered a slur on my reputation; but as he is dead and Dance is alive, I will not quote his actual words on the subject. Anyhow, I played the part and the composer was delighted; whether the author was or was

Photograph   Russell & Sons

THE RAJAH OF CHUTNEYPORE, IN "NAUTCH GIRL."

not I never heard, but in any case I won half the battle.

During the two foregoing London seasons I had been playing some original musical duologues to which my prolific friend Solomon had also supplied the music, in company with my little comrade Jessie Bond, who was gifted with a personality which made her a universal favourite, and we had formed an impression that a provincial tour would be both amusing and profitable.

I accordingly arranged one with Vert, the well-known agent, for that autumn, we being very kindly released by Carte for three months on the distinct understanding that we then resumed our parts.

The little tour was a great artistic success, which gratified me the more as I had written all the little pieces myself, but we came to the conclusion that the provinces were no gold mine, and the first trip was also the last. One of our worst houses was at Barnard Castle, where the intelligent local agent had recommended the day of the annual flower show and fireworks. There were only three reserved seats taken, so I hastily requisitioned the services of the town crier, who went all round the place announcing that the entertainment was postponed, and we attended the fireworks ourselves. This was the only occasion on the tour when we turned away money.

During my absence from the Savoy my part of the Rajah was taken over by Penley, as great a physical contrast to me as could well be imagined, not to mention the difference in method.   He told me that he did not feel very happy in the part, and I found it easy to believe on hearing that on one evening some rude person in the gallery interrupted him in the middle of a speech and inquired loudly, "Where's Barrington?"   Penley turned to one of his comrades on the stage and remarked plaintively, "I'm having a rosy time of it, ain't I?"   I should rather expect something of the same sort to happen if I were to make my appearance as Charley's Aunt, which I do not mean to do.

Courtice Pounds had a very good part in this piece, which he invested with the charm he brings to all his work, and I used never to tire of listening to his solo when in prison, followed by a very catchy duet with Jessie Bond, their voices blending particularly well.   Pounds was also very popular as the smug curate in *The Vicar of Bray*.   He used to say that when playing in *The Gondoliers*, in which his part and mine were so closely associated as to be a kind of duet, he felt he must develop a stronger vein of comedy, to keep level, as it were, and there is no doubt that he did improve in his acting enormously from that time, and I think put the seal on his fame by his delightful rendering of the Clown in *Twelfth Night* with Tree some few years ago.

The latter end of this year saw me back at the Savoy, where I once more took up my part of the Rajah, and we also began the rehearsals for *Haddon Hall*.

Photograph   Alfred Ellis

RUPERT VERNON, IN "HADDON HALL."

Still another combination of author and composer was tried in this piece, in the hopes of wooing a return of some of our former glory. I believe it to have been Sydney Grundy's first flight into the realms of opera, and he could hardly have chosen a more attractive theme or one more likely to appeal to Arthur Sullivan.

Grundy has always appealed to me as the typical John Bull kind of man, and when he told me he was going to spend a fortnight or so with Sullivan in the south of France in order to arrange the sequence of musical numbers and other matters, I could not refrain from expressing my surprise and anxiety as to his diet. He had evidently had the same fear himself, for he answered at once, "Sullivan guarantees English cookery"; but all the same, he confessed on his return that he would infinitely rather have spent the same time with Sullivan in London. There was, of course, some very beautiful music in *Haddon Hall*, and Rosina Brandram's song, "Queen of the Garden" and the duet "Friendship," in which she was joined by Richard Green, were two gems. I always felt that my part in this play was a kind of excrescence, being in fact written because I was there, and possibly wanted there; but it should really have been the villain of the plot, and a serious rival to Courtice Pounds in the love interest, instead of a would-be humorous combination of the two.

Haddon Hall had not been running long when the welcome news flew round the Press that we were to once more find our Utopia with the two original magicians, who were engaged on a work bearing that title, and sure enough we were duly summoned to a reading.

This was fixed for a Monday, and I had been spending my week-end at Ryde, and to my intense annoyance the boat-train was late and threatened to make me unpunctual. I sent a long explanatory telegram from Mitcham Junction begging them not to wait, but found to my chagrin, on arriving about half an hour behind time, that Gilbert had most kindly insisted on waiting for me. Both Sullivan and Carte abused me heartily for "daring" to be late and keep Gilbert waiting, and seemed to think I ought either to have got out and run or never gone away at all. It was rather amusing, as after all the call was the author's special call, and he was quite charming about it.

We had a fresh importation for this opera in the person of Miss McIntosh, who played the principal soprano, and imported a great amount of delicacy and refinement to the rôle of the Princess Zara, qualities which gave additional point to the Utopian dreams it was her duty in the part to voice.

Although a success, it did not achieve one of the old-fashioned Savoy runs, and I rather incline to think that this may have been in some measure due to the second act, which was not as full of fun as usual; indeed, a great part of it was taken up with the realization of a "drawing-room" with the

THE KING OF UTOPIA.

presentations made in due form, and perhaps it may
have been a trifle tedious. It was great fun for the
company on the days when we had a lady professor
of deportment attending rehearsals to teach us how
to bow. I believe there was also a certain amount
of friction in a very high quarter over the fact that
when dressed as a field-marshal and wearing an order
confined to a very select few, I took part in a species
of nigger-minstrel number which was rounded off
with a breakdown. There was a very bright young
baritone named Scott Fishe, who had the part of
a financier and sang a song about " The English
Girl," which in my humble opinion was one of
Gilbert's best efforts. Denny, John le Hay, and
myself, also had a very excellent dancing trio in the
second act, and le Hay was quite admirable all
through the play ; indeed, the more I think about
it the less I understand why it did not run longer.

Utopia was, after all, not to prove the recommence-
ment of a series, and Gilbert and Sullivan drifted
apart once more at the end of it, and again we had
to fall back on extraneous talent. This time Carte
appeared to desire something quite out of the beaten
track, and the result was a very weird piece indeed
written by J. M. Barrie and Conan Doyle, to which
Ernest Ford supplied some very excellent music. I
have never to this day been able to discover with
certitude what it was all about, and the title *Jane
Annie* can hardly be described as illuminating, at least
to the average mind, whatever it may be to the thinker.

The second act was full of allusions to golf, and the scene was actually laid on a golf green, and the whole thing seemed to puzzle our audiences very much, golf not being in those days the well-known factor in life which it now is. The best part in the piece was a caddie, and only one or two of us knew what a caddie was. I myself played a Proctor, and, for some reason which I have forgotten, hid myself in a clock, a most uncomfortable position always, and especially so one night when I sneezed violently and my spectacles, which formed the hands, fell off.

The whole Savoy company went out on tour with this opera, and I am bound to say that they seemed to know more about it in the provinces.

Ernest Ford went with us as musical director, and he, Scott Fishe, Kenningham, and myself generally stayed in the same house, being all four keen golfers; and I remember being much amused at our landlady in Birmingham, who stared in amazement at our bags of clubs on arrival, and exclaimed, " Bless my soul! what are them fakemajerkers ? " It struck me as such a lovely word that I have never forgotten it. After we had been three days in her house, and I had collected my golfers each morning about nine and gone off for the day, she said to me, " Well, I've never seen such a queer lot of actors." I asked her what complaint she wished to make, when she replied, " Complaint! I likes yer. All the actor folk who comes to me lies in bed till two o'clock in the day! You're no trouble at all—it's a 'oliday for me." And

Photograph   Alfred Ellis

THE PROCTOR, IN "JANE ANNIE"

nothing was too good for us for the whole of that week.

We had an extraordinary and almost incredible experience in Bradford one night with Scott Fishe. He and Kenningham had deserted golf for one day to take part in a cricket match against a team that I described with would-be humour as Licentious Victuallers, and when Ford and I returned from golf we found each of them fast asleep on sofas in the sitting-room. So far so good; but it shortly became time to go to the theatre, and though we eventually aroused Kenningham, nothing we could do would waken Scott Fishe. He could not be left—time was flying—so between us we half carried, half pushed him round the corner, got him dressed, and stood by him till his cue came to go on the stage, and literally shoved him on. He went through the dialogue of his scene, sang his song without making the slightest mistake, came off the stage and—*woke up!* not having a notion what he had done.

G

VIII

OUR hopes of a continuance of the partnership were doomed to disappointment, and there was no opera to follow *Utopia,* and Gilbert cast about for a new home, manager, and composer, which he eventually found in the Lyric Theatre, George Edwardes, and Osmond Carr, resulting in the production of *His Excellency.*

This was a gallant attempt at transplanting the laurels grown at the Savoy, and was supported by Ellaline Terriss, Jessie Bond, Nancy McIntosh, le Hay, Kenningham, and myself, and was also memorable to me for the renewal of association with my old friend George Grossmith, after a lengthy severance. We much enjoyed coming together again, but it proved to be for the last time.

The centre of the stage in the first act was occupied with a statue of myself as the Regent, of the size called, I believe, heroic, and in order to have this executed with the thoroughness so essential in everything with which Gilbert is connected, I had to give a number of sittings to the well-known

Photograph   Alfred Ellis & Walery.

THE REGENT, IN "HIS EXCELLENCY" (ACT I.)

sculptor Lucchesi. The first few of these sittings interested me tremendously, but as the novelty gradually wore off I found it extremely difficult to keep awake. Fortunately, as Lucchesi remarked, my face, awake or asleep, was very much the same, and he was not obliged to reproduce the snore. Anyhow, it was a most effective statue, and he kindly presented me with a cast of the head as a souvenir. I had a terrible bout of rheumatism during the run of this piece, and for nearly a fort-night used to go to work in a four-wheeler, from which I was almost carried to my dressing-room and then vigorously massaged before I could move; but once on the stage, most of the stiffness left me even if the pain did not.

There was nothing particularly distinguished in the music of the opera, and it did not achieve a very long run, though extremely successful at first.

I remember going to see Grossmith in his room one evening and finding a visitor with him—a coloured gentleman, whose name I did not catch on introduction, but whom I found a very pleasant fellow indeed. After he left I inquired of Grossmith his name, and was astonished to hear that it was Peter Jackson. This was my first introduction to the Ring.

This engagement was also memorable to me as being the occasion of the production of a one-act romantic piece of my own writing, called *The Knight Errant*, for which Alfred Caldicott wrote some delightful music, and my old friend Percy Anderson designed some effective dresses, especially one for the Crusader.

It was fairly successful, but I used to be horribly annoyed at a laugh from the audience at a certain line in a serious situation, which came invariably. I could not understand why it was so, and we tried the line every way possible, with the same result. At last I cut it out completely, and went to hear the piece that night full of hope; but the laugh came as before, and I never saw the piece again, have no copy of it, and do not know where the music has gone. See what a laugh may do to an author.

The only other time Grossmith and myself were playing in the same theatre was shortly after the conclusion of the run of *His Excellency*, and the cause of our reunion was the illness of poor old Johnnie Toole, who was playing in a piece by Ralph Lumley, called *Thoroughbred*, at his own theatre. The dear old fellow had not been playing in it for long before he was attacked with the illness which necessitated a retirement which was to prove permanent. He was in a dilemma what to do with his company and theatre, when it was suggested to him that he should engage me for his part, and get Grossmith to give one of his musical sketches to wind up the evening. I had several delightful interviews with Toole, who was then at Hastings, and looking forward quite cheerily to his reappearance, though, as he wrote me in a letter referring to the matter, his writing was nearly as weak as his knees.

The second act took place on a race-course, presumably Ascot, and almost the whole of the tiny stage was taken up with a real coach. Nevertheless it seemed to me that we wanted more people to make some kind of excitement as a race was supposed to flash by, and I suggested to Toole that a few supers would be useful for the purpose. He wrote in answer, " Do as you like, of course, but I never found a super draw a postage stamp."

The great hit of the piece was in this act, where myself and two other characters were disguised as nigger minstrels (I was supposed to be there unknown to my wife, who was on the coach), and we sang a song written by George Grossmith, called " Keep the baby warm, mother."

It used to get rapturous encores, and I feel certain that if we had supplemented it with a few really bad riddles and another song or two, we should have been playing the piece now, and Charing Cross Hospital would never have been enlarged.

I believe Toole to have been the first to christen a theatre with a personal name, a custom I venture to think not a sound one, as it identifies it too strongly with one artist, and unless that artist is appearing there is a sense of deprivation. This, of course, only applies to eminent names, and " The Gladys," or

" The Phyllis," or " The Jim " might be all right, but I think nothing could be really better than the use of the street in which the house is situated.

I rather fancy that although disappointed for many reasons from a business point of view, dear old Toole was secretly rather pleased that we were unable to keep his theatre open for any great length of time.

I saw him at long intervals almost up to the time of his death, and he was always cheerful, and when almost past seeing and hearing would inquire on every occasion that brought him to town, " What theatre do we go to to-night ? "

The only Gilbert and Sullivan opera in which I did not appear was one of the most successful and most beautiful, *The Yeomen of the Guard*, produced during my occupation of the St. James's Theatre, and it has always been a source of regret to me that I should have missed one of the series of triumphs, and one in which a part was absolutely written for me, though I doubt if I should have made as good a gaoler as Denny, the creator of the part, and who looked it to the life.

The traditional excellence of the Savoy concerted numbers was, if possible, more than usual in evidence in this piece, which abounds with ear-haunting melodies. And what a part is Jack Point ! I should like to see an actor of the type of Joseph Jefferson play it.

While playing in *Thoroughbred* at Toole's, I began

Photograph *Alfred Ellis*

Strephon, in "Happy Arcadia." (German Reed Entertainment.)

to wonder whether I had for ever cut myself adrift from musical work, but at the conclusion of the run I found I had not, as I was persuaded to join in an attempt to keep alive the glories of the German Reed entertainment at the St. George's Hall, which had some little time previously collapsed owing to the lamentable deaths of Alfred Reed and Corney Grain.

The loss of these two popular entertainers was the more to be regretted as after a long spell of only moderate success, fortune was just commencing to be more lavish of her favours. This was owing to the fact that Grain had been persuaded to resume his parts in the sketches instead of confining himself entirely to a piano monologue.

Even here I was not to be dissociated from Gilbert, as the piece chosen for our opening bill was *Happy Arcadia*, in which I appeared as Strephon and dragged a woolly lamb round with me, which I hated. I was anxious to have continued the run of *Melodramania*, which was going so very strongly when so fatally interrupted, but I was outvoted on the council, owing, I believe, to some sentimental feeling of opposition.

The German Reed orchestra was an odd contrast to what I had been accustomed to, but it had one great advantage—it was not nearly so easy to drown the singer.

One of my own duologues formed the centre of the programme, in which I played a sham professor of hypnotism, rather like a part played by Willie Edouin some few years later.

We went the usual autumn tour of the south coast towns, and the place of Fanny Holland was filled by my old Opera Comique colleague, Emily Cross. The presence of such an old friend made the tour a great pleasure, but it was none too successful; indeed, I think we were rather looked askance at by the public, as usurping a title to which we had no real right, and I believe we should have been wiser to drop the German Reed Entertainment headline to our announcements, the glamour of it having departed with Reed and Grain, never to return.

At the conclusion of the tour I returned to town, and to my great surprise and pleasure was offered a part in a new opera by Gilbert and Sullivan, to be produced at the Savoy. This was indeed good news, and I once more looked forward to a renewal of the old days, to be inaugurated with *The Grand Duke*, which, however, turned out to be the last work of the famous collaborators.

By this time much of the all-English atmosphere, which in former days had been so strenuously insisted on, had evaporated, so it was no surprise to find in our new *prima donna* a foreigner who was reputed to have taken high rank in her profession in her own country, though I never found out if this was earned entirely by her artistic capabilities, or enhanced to a certain extent by the fact of her being Countess Ilka von Palmay.

THE PROFESSOR. (GERMAN REED ENTERTAINMENT.)

The veriest glutton for work might have been satisfied with my part in this opera, about the longest and most hard-working I have ever undertaken, and yet one in which I failed to find too many chances of scoring. At the early rehearsals it seemed to me that I was "on" all the time with the exception of one scene of Madame Palmay's, and then one morning Gilbert informed me that he had brought me into this scene also. It was a kind of mad scene, which she played very well, and it was most effective, so I naturally felt rather gratified, but the feeling diminished to a certain extent when I found that my part in it was to consist chiefly in being dragged about the stage by my wig and generally banged about. However, I went most conscientiously to work on it, and one night I elicited a great laugh by escaping from the infuriated madwoman and dodging about behind some pillars. This, however, did not strike the fair artist as humorously as it did myself and the audience, and I was requested for the future to take my punishment lying down, so to speak. Some people like all the fun to themselves.

July 18th, 1896, was the night of my last appearance at my old home, and towards the end of August in the same year I found myself launched on the troubled waters of musical comedy, the captain of the ship being that astute caterer for the public amusement, George Edwardes, whom I had first met in the employ of Carte, and who was now well on the road to fame and fortune as a manager; and with him I remained, with the exception of one or two brief intervals, until the production of *The Michus*, for which opera he considered it wise for some, to us, inscrutable reason to disband his old company, and from the success of the piece I imagine that he cannot have missed any of us more than we have possibly missed him.

Apart from the large number of artists who, at one time or another, appeared at the Savoy, it would seem that all the stage hands of all the London theatres have had a spell there too, for in every theatre I have played or do play in, and also in the music halls, I invariably see some face I know, and on greeting its owner am equally invariably greeted with the remark, " Well, guv'nor, we haven't met since the old Savoy days; glad to see you looking so well "—a meeting that always brings me a feeling of pleasure with a touch of sadness in it.

How many people could produce two pieces at the same time, I wonder, and not get them hopelessly tangled ?   And yet this used to be simple relaxation for George Edwardes in those days, and he would only consider himself working if, in addition to Daly's and the Gaiety, there were a new ballet at the Empire and a farcical comedy somewhere else to manipulate. He could set a scene, too, as well as rehearse one, and I shall never forget the first night of the Country Girl, the second act of which consisted mainly of a huge staircase, about half of which was not in the theatre at all.   There was a fearful wait, and when

I came down to commence the act, I found George
with his coat off·helping the stage hands and shouting his directions, and I believe 'he was absolutely
"discovered" when the curtain finally rose. The
audience was naturally very impatient, but he set
everything right with a short speech at the end of
the evening. I have seldom met a man with a
happier knack of saying the right thing in a few
words, whether the thing to be said is pleasant or
the reverse, though, to do him justice, when the
latter is the case, the obligation to speak is usually
handed on to one of his lieutenants, and with justice,
or why employ them? There is to my mind a kind
of atmosphere at Daly's which impresses you on
taking your seat with·the idea that you are going
to get better entertainment there than at most other
places, and much of this is due to the strong personality of the presiding genius, and a stronger it would
be difficult to imagine. I have known his really
genuine geniality employed with such effect to an
unwelcome, and perhaps aggressive, caller, as to leave
that person at the close of the interview with the
impression that George is his best friend and well-
wisher, and this happy conclusion is arrived at with-
out·the caller having uttered one word of what he
came to say. I fancy the diplomatic career would
have been eminently suitable to him not only for the
above reason, but also because of his fondness for
entertaining and natural qualities as a host; he
keeps open house at home, and at restaurants

you will never see him dining with less than one guest.

He was naturally always on the look-out for fresh talent, and many a young artist owes his or her tuition in singing or dancing to "The Chief," as we used to call him. One day at rehearsal a very diminutive child was brought to dance to him, which she did extremely well and to George's great satisfaction. "Really, it's wonderful—splendid!" Then turning to the child's escort, he asked, "What's the age of your little daughter?" "Not my daughter—sister—twenty-eight." The Chief's face was a sight.

Rehearsals at Daly's were always extremely lengthy affairs, partly owing to the number of people who had suggestions to offer, but more to the fact that many of the scenes were written and rewritten at the moment. In one opera I made my first entrance late in Act I, and for a whole week I attended from about twelve to four without once being called upon to do anything. But I was not singular in this, as in *The Cingalee* there were some half-dozen ladies who formed what was christened for short "The English Party," and who, after being there hours at a time for a fortnight, heard with mingled feelings the announcement, "The English Party can go." However, their turn came later, and hours were spent over the one number in which they were prominently concerned, and which after the first night was cut bodily out.

IX

WHEN first making acquaintance with the irresponsibilities of what is popularly known as musical comedy, I felt a certain sense of insecurity, owing to the absence of boundary marks in the shape of lines written by the author, and I believe that for quite a year or so I shocked a great many of my fellow-artists by the tenacity with which I clung to the "text." This, of course, was due to my Savoy training, and to this day even I am occasionally conscious of a guilty feeling when making a gag, and find myself looking round to see if the author is anywhere at hand.

The beginning of my long stay with George Edwardes was marked in an unostentatious manner by my appearance in the *Gaiety Girl* at Eastbourne. This was done to meet my wishes, as I wanted a few weeks to get into the part before appearing in it at Daly's. There were a few lines in the piece which I fancy could not have had much margin in escaping the eye of the Licenser of Plays, some of them being in my part, and I was rather upset when the local manager came to see me, just before the curtain rang up, to tell me of what he evidently considered a great compliment paid me by the heads of two of the largest schools for young ladies for which Eastbourne is so famous, this being that each proprietress had booked a large number of seats because " Mr. Rutland Barrington's name on the programme was a guarantee that they could safely bring the young ladies." What I had done to deserve such an excellent reputation I am not quite aware, and I have never paid a return visit to see whether it is forfeited or not. On relating this incident to the author, he greatly consoled me by saying that in all probability the significance of the lines in question would be entirely lost on the old ladies unless explained by their pupils.

After visiting a few more coast towns, of which Yarmouth alone stands out with any vividness on account of its excellent golf links, I took up the part at Daly's, where I had the pleasure of being associated with Lottie Venne, Mrs. Phelps, Hayden Coffin, Fred Kaye, and others too numerous to mention. There was a revival of this play in later years in which, owing to " existing contracts," I suffered the mortification of seeing my old part, in which I had been so successful, none too well-handled by an artist who was physically unfitted to play it. I myself played the Judge, a part which, when I first joined the company, was being admirably rendered by my old friend Eric Lewis. The play which followed this was *The Artist's Model*, and as it had been written before I joined the company, there was no part in it for me, so I was again thrown back to the "legitimate" in the shape of a revival of *The Mikado* at the Savoy.

There had been one of the periodical sort of public outcries for a Gilbert and Sullivan revival, and it seemed to promise success, as most of the old cast was available. I did not look forward with any special pleasure to my reappearance as Pooh Bah, as I had got rather tired of the part during the long original run, and my forebodings were realized, as after playing it for a month or so I began to feel as if I had never played anything else, and it so worked on my brain that I felt compelled to ask Carte to release me, which he very kindly did, and within a very short time I returned to Daly's for *The Geisha*, which play was the commencement of a stay of ten years with George Edwardes.

Oddly enough, my engagement this time also commenced with a few weeks on tour, as I rehearsed a week at Plymouth and then opened in Birmingham. Being anxious to have a companion on this tour who was a good golfer, I suggested to Herbert Ross that he should join the company. It seemed to strike him as a happy idea, so I sent him to interview George Edwardes, who said, " I hear you want to go on this *Geisha* golf tour with Barrington?" Ross expressed his desire to do so, and was forthwith engaged. On asking what part he was to play, George replied, " Oh, there's no part;

you'd better see the stage manager," which he did, and it ended with his strolling on with the other naval officers and chipping in with a line when he saw a chance. Within a week or so he suggested to two of these officers that certain of their lines were quite unsuited to their personal appearance, and that they would be wise to surrender them to him. They actually did this, and eventually his part was quite a good combination of all the best lines from the others added to his own inventions. There are not many actors who could play such a game as this on their fellow-artists, and there are fewer still who can play a better game than Ross at his best. His golf was naturally rather expensive to me, but it worked out about quits with the piquet which we played during our journeys and waits. We were a rather strong combination in a foursome, and many of the clubs we visited used to put up couples against us who almost invariably contributed to our weekly hotel bills in liberal fashion.

Roland Cunningham was also with us on this tour, but at that time had not taken up golf, but we have had many happy days at it of late years.

We had a tenor with us who was rather an oddity in his way, even for a tenor, though he certainly had a most sympathetic voice and sang with great charm and finish. He always dressed to look rather like one's boyhood's idea of an Italian bravo, and his slouch hats were the admiration of the passer-by.

He had quaint ideas too, for not so very long since he was invited to play the part of Defendant in *Trial by Jury* for some great benefit, and on attending the first music call declined to attend the stage-rehearsals. When remonstrated with he said, "You can inform Mr. Gilbert that I will study the music, and playing the part cannot present any difficulty to an artist who has played Lohengrin." I presume it did, however, as some one else played the part.

On arriving at my dressing-room in Glasgow one Monday, I found to my alarm and annoyance that it reeked with some overwhelming odour—(this is many years ago, and the theatre has since been thoroughly overhauled)—and naturally demanded to be moved; but it was the " star " room, and there was nowhere to move me to. I foraged around and discovered the possibility of screening off a portion of the very large property-room. This was done, and I was feeling happier, when the dresser who looked after the tenor aforesaid appeared with a polite request that he might join me, having been put into the room I had vacated. Of course I consented, but as his presence cramped me I cast about for some means to be rid of him. On consulting Herbert Ross, he came to the conclusion that the best plan to gain my object would be to secure a supply of some even worse odour than the one we had fled from, and with the assistance of the property master this was done. On arriving the next night I was greeted with a smell that you could absolutely have hung a hat on!

H

What it had been done with I never knew, but it was innocuous and cost half a crown, and I am certain no one ever bought so much smell so cheaply. When the tenor arrived his face was a sight to watch (there were several of us doing it). He yelled out, "My God, I shall die!" seized his clothes and made a dash for the room he had previously declared unfit for a dog, but in which he gladly remained for the rest of the week, and consoled himself by prophesying all kinds of complaints for me.

I laugh at this even now when I think about it; but when I told the story for the first time, to my intense surprise it did not go at all well. This was on the following Sunday, when we went to Edinburgh, and a dear old friend of mine, Walter Hatton, gave a dinner party to about six other men to meet me, and I told this true history as an after-dinner story, but to my dismay it was received with a chilly silence. When his guests had gone I asked Walter Hatton if he could offer any explanation, He said he could think of none, except, perhaps, that they might have felt it a little personal, being all of them directors of the theatre in question.

It was during this visit to Edinburgh that I made the acquaintance of the Law family, the head of which is the present proprietor of *The Scotsman.* Some of the happiest weeks of my life have been spent at their summer residence, Archerfield House, which possesses within the estate its own delightful golf-links, where one can play nine holes out to sea, bathe,

Photograph   Alfred Ellis & Walery.

YEN HOW, IN "SAN TOY."

and play the second nine in to breakfast, lunch, or dinner as suits the mood of the player. It was on this course that Tait and Hilton played a very memorable match, Hilton going round in seventy-four and not winning one single hole.

A peculiarity of the parts I played in both *The Gaiety Girl* and *The Geisha* was that there were no songs in either and remarkably little concerted music. This was owing to the fact that they were written for Monkhouse, who was supposed not to be a singer, though I well recollect his joining in a duet with Ada Jenoure in Gilbert's *Mountebanks* at the Lyric Theatre.

San Toy was the next Daly production, and whether the polygamous leanings of the Marquis Imari in *The Geisha* suggested the idea to the author, or for some other unexplained reason, I know not, but I was doomed in this piece to the possession of "six little wives," and the idea worked out so successfully that for the remainder of my career with George Edwardes I was fated to play the bigamist—fortunately for me without any of the penalties or pleasures attaching to the position. I am not sure that this continual harping on one, or rather six strings, was not just a trifle monotonous for the audience, and I once remonstrated with George Edwardes on the similarity of my parts and the narrow scope they afforded, to which he replied, "They don't mind what you do, Rutty, as long as they just see you." This sounded very complimentary but did not abso-

lutely console me, and I have found since leaving
him that on having more, and more varied, work in
plays I have appeared in the public has been kind
enough to show a decided appreciation of the change.
There is no manner of doubt whatever that an artist
may stay too long with one management, but it is a
difficult thing to avoid in face of the undoubted
pleasure the public has in welcoming the same cast
in piece after piece.

From my own case I can support this theory by
the fact that I was frequently asked, " Are you not
at the Savoy ? " for some year or two after I had
severed the connection. I heard of an actor who
met George Edwardes in the street one day, stopped
and spoke to him, and George said, " Come and see
me, my dear boy—I think I can find you a part,"
and he was much astonished when the actor replied,
" Why, Mr. Edwardes, I've been with you at the
Gaiety for the last six years ! "

San Toy was the first piece in which I suggested
the advisability of my having a topical song, an idea
which appealed at once to George, with the result
that I had one in every piece that followed. Adrian
Ross very kindly used to consult me as to the refrain,
by far the most important feature of these songs, and
having fixed upon something we hoped would prove
catchy, he would write an introductory verse or two,
and the rest was left to me. I was extremely fortunate in possessing the faculty of writing verses about
people or things of immediate or transitory interest,

the great advantage of the gift being that if one has
to wait until supplied by the recognized author of the
lyrics, the topic was frequently stale before the verse
came to hand.   Adrian Ross paid me the unsolicited
compliment of publishing my name with his in connection with all these songs, but in spite of that
people even now express surprise when I tell them
that my topical verses are my own unaided efforts.
I was once taken to task by a—it could not have
been " the "—dramatic critic of a world-famous half-
penny paper for what he was pleased to consider a
fault of ignorance.   I was singing a verse during the
visit of the King and Queen of Portugal to London,
in which I, of course purposely, rhymed " frugal "
with " Portoogal," so much to the amusement of His
Majesty that he did me the honour of sending for a
copy of the verse after hearing it.   The aforesaid
critic wrote in his paper : " The poet of Daly's must
have been very hard up for a rhyme in this instance
—perhaps he will allow me to suggest ' sort-o'-gal ' as
avoiding such dreadful mispronunciation."

I wrote to the editor about this young man, but
received no reply, so I assume that he at least had a
sense of humour.

San Toy, as was the case with most of the Daly
productions, required a tremendous amount of rehearsing, and I have always found that when this is
the case it results in a greater amount of friction
between author, actor, and stage-manager than is
usual when things shape quickly.   This friction is

frequently increased by, if not perhaps wholly attributable to, the presence of one or more personal friends
of the manager who assume the privilege of making
suggestions.   When you take into consideration the
facts that, as a general rule, the modern producer
comes to his task without any too firmly developed
ideas as to what he wishes the principal artists to do
(trusting to rehearsals to unfold possibilities), and in
some cases also lacking the capacity to assist the said
artists ; and that all artists have an inclination to
look upon suggestions which concern themselves as
almost puerile and certainly ineffective, it is somewhat marvellous that these musical comedies arrive
at a production at all.   In the whole of my career I
have only known one man perfectly qualified to
point the way they should go to all concerned, from
principal to chorus, and that one is W. S. Gilbert.
Of course, I am dealing only with the musical branch
of the stage, but I have an impression that Pinero,
Sydney Grundy, and Cecil Raleigh, among the play-
wrights, may be set down as *proxime accesserunt* if
not *æquales*.

Edwardes determined to have a " reading " of *San
Toy* to the company—an innovation at Daly's; and I
well remember the nervousness of the author.   He
was still further disconcerted when, Act I having
been received with " modified rapture," after Act II
had been in progress some five minutes, a certain line
drew a very hearty laugh, greeted by George with
the remark, " Bravo, Morton!   That's the first laugh."

The natural obstacle to a reading of the pieces was
the fact that huge portions of them were written
either during rehearsal or after leaving off, in time
for the next day, this being not so much the fault of
the author as owing to the objections that George
would take to certain scenes, and as very few of his
objections were overruled—he being both Steward
and Jockey Club—these scenes had perforce to go
by the board and fresh ones be written. This occasionally tangled the story considerably; but however
much it distressed the author, it did not so affect
George, who had about this time developed a strong
antagonism to "plot." On one occasion it necessitated a totally different line being wanted, and
George appealed to the artist—no use; the stage
manager—no; then to me—no; when he finally
turned to the author and said most genially,
"Morton, can't you think of a line?" However,
with all these troubles *San Toy* eventually proved
one of our biggest successes, even though that delightful and wonderful artist Marie Tempest did not
feel quite happy in the title rôle; indeed, she left us
before very long, and was replaced by a very charming little San Toy in Florence Collingbourne.

Later on, by way of a marked contrast, the part
was played by Ada Reeve, who certainly surmounted
in a very clever way the difficulties presented by a
character so diametrically opposed to her method and
personality. Fred Kaye had a very long speech to
deliver on one of his entrances, which gave the Chief

a lot of trouble and cause for consideration. After trying it all kinds of ways without success, he took a moment for silent thought, and suddenly exclaimed: "I've got it, Freddy! You just come on hurriedly, walk to the middle of the stage, and say 'What!'" It was left at that.

On one occasion I determined to sing as many encores of "Introduce it into China" as the audience would allow. They amounted, including two introductory lines, to eleven verses, and I honestly believe they would have stood more, but I had not got them.

I have one very charming personal recollection in connection with *San Toy*. The occasion was a great reception given to the C.I.V., on their return from the war, by the Artists' Corps, who numbered many of them, and of which Corps my old friend Brandon Thomas was an officer. I wrote a special song on the C.I.V. for the occasion, and Florence Collingbourne kindly sang it. One of the gallant warriors was introduced to her at the concert, and they were shortly afterwards married.

X

MUSICAL COMEDY—"GREEK SLAVE"—"COUNTRY GIRL"

MUSICAL COMEDY is a title that appears to me to have been invented to describe a type of piece that generally has too little of the latter and too much of the former in its composition to make for its being a thoroughly well-balanced affair, though in spite of that it has undoubtedly increased the balances of many of its producers, while at the same time upsetting the equilibrium of many of the artists concerned in it.

Owing to these conflicting influences it is regarded by many as a hybrid which threatens grave danger to the cause of Art; they continually predict its decease, but it continues to flourish exceedingly. The great difficulty which its manufacturers have to contend with appears to be the initial one of finding a good plot, which must be strong enough to bear total elimination during rehearsal, and still leave an aroma, so to speak, powerful enough to suggest to the audience that it was in evidence at one time. This process of exhaustion has been successfully adopted by the makers for many years without always leaving their patrons in a state of bewilderment, as there is undoubtedly a large section of playgoers who thoroughly enjoy a piece without any overwhelming desire to know what it is about. Owen Hall, I fancy, was the originator of this class of entertainment, and having played in most of his pieces, I had opportunities of condoling with him in the matter of his disappearing plots. One striking instance, and one which, I think justifiably, upset him immensely, was in a play of his in which the *clou* was the discovery of an eminent philanthropist supping with a music-hall artist, *in camera*, by the philanthropist's wife—not perhaps a very new, but always a very successful situation—the effect of which was entirely destroyed by the conversion of the wife into four daughters! There were great complications between one of the Oriental Potentates I played at Daly's and his English wife, all of which disappeared in less than a fortnight after production, the wife being handed over to another husband without any appeal to the Divorce Court. Possibly the contributors who suffered least were the writers of the lyrics, such work as that furnished by Adrian Ross and Harry Greenbank retaining its place unchallenged by the exigencies of plot, the main difficulty in their case being to find some variant of the inevitable " Bird " song for the soubrette and the " Animal " duet for her and the low comedian which seemed indispensable. The music is naturally a great factor in these successes, but even that is subject to the same process of elimination ; and in one case of a play which ran nearly two years, the composer told me that, with the exception of the finale to Act I, there was not a bar of his music left in.   Good tunes from all sources are annexed—legally, of course—and dropped like plums into the pudding with, in some instances, most incongruous effects, such as, for example, a coon duet with moonlight effect on the square of St. Mark's, Venice, in the full blaze of day! Certain of the music-makers, I imagine, are somewhat distressed at these incongruities, and with reason when one considers the claims of such composers as Sydney Jones, Ivan Caryll, Lionel Monckton, and Leslie Stuart, to mention only a few, though on consideration I am inclined to think the first-named the more fortunate in not having had to deal with the later and still more invertebrate form of piece. Many of the most important manufacturers are to be found among the player folk who appear in these plays, some of whom write a great part of their parts, and all of whom graft their own humour, both of words and business, on the parent tree as provided by the eight or ten authors employed. Notable examples of this kind of work are G. P. Huntley, George Graves, Huntley Wright, Fred Kaye, George Barrett, Payne, Ethel Irving, and poor Willie Edouin, perhaps the best of all, and who gave us in *Hoggenheimer* a performance humorous enough to rank with anything by anybody, in which he was more than ably seconded by Ethel Irving, the two personalities making largely for the success of the piece.

Paul Rubens is another prominent musical-comedy maker who, having served a novitiate in providing and inventing many delicious little entrées as one of George Edwardes's army of *chefs*, has now blossomed into the furnisher of entire menus. The accepted and acceptable mannerism of certain artists, while undoubtedly making much of the success of these plays, has undoubtedly its dangerous side, as with the artists in question absent from the cast the commercial side of the venture is apt to suffer.

It also has a naturally bad effect on the unfortunate understudy, who is allowed very little latitude for his or her personal intelligence or ability, and has perforce to model himself or herself on the prototype, with frequently disastrous elimination of all individuality.

Producers of these plays are practically in line with authors as manufacturers, a position which they have arrogated to the extent of establishing it as customary. This is, of course, no drawback when such "producers" are George Edwardes, Curzon, Courtneidge, and men of their kind who have experience to guide them, but there is pain and grief in store in abundance for the author and composer who have the misfortune (as I have) to have placed a piece with a manager who does not know A flat from a bull's foot, and yet has the good taste to ignore suggestions from a competent person.

My old friend Willie Ward has, in an unobtrusive way, a good deal to do with the Daly productions, inventing much of the business for the chorus and all the dancing, which he teaches himself, besides presenting little character sketches in the various plays, all carefully thought out, and for which, in the case of foreign parts, the Museum is laid under contribution. His devil-dance in *The Cingalee* was a striking example of getting a big effect with little real exertion. I know this because, though he seemed to be putting in "all he knew," I had my suspicions, and taxed him with it. He replied at once, "You are quite right, it's a fake!" but it was a fake that took a Willie Ward to engineer.

There was a gallant attempt made in one piece I played in to get nearer the true form of comedy, one of the features being the absence of a chorus, but within a few weeks this invisible feature disappeared under the advent of additional sailors and waitresses, and I heard that in their next production the chorus were more in evidence than ever.

During the run of *San Toy* I had the very unpleasant experience of being late for my work. This has only happened to me twice in all my career; I have naturally had many narrow shaves, but only twice have I absolutely failed to arrive in time. I was coming up from Deal, being due at Daly's for *San Toy* about 8.15. I had played two rounds of golf before leaving Deal at 3.41, and slept peacefully in the train until I was waked at London Bridge and asked for my ticket. I handed it over, and told the collector that they should keep their clocks in better order. He replied, "That's the right time, sir, 8.45!" And it was, and I ought to have been on the stage with my six little wives. On arriving, I suggested to the stage manager that I might as well go home, but he persuaded me to play the rest of the part; so as one man had already been on for the Marquis, I alluded to myself for the rest of the evening as "we," which afforded amusement to the members of the orchestra, if to no one else. These little items are all they have to relieve the monotony of their evening, and I have personally always found the orchestra a splendid audience.

The other occasion on which I was late was during the run of *Patience*, and this time the South-Western was in fault. I was spending a Bank Holiday afternoon at Harry Chinnery's pretty place by Teddington Weir, and Gilbert was of the party. When I took my leave at five o'clock he suggested that I was going very early. I reminded him of what travelling was likely to be on such a day, and he agreed it was as well to have a margin. The train left Teddington all right at 5.30, but I arrived at the Savoy after nine, and yet it did not break down. Margins are no use with trains, and I shall never forget the horrible feeling of impatience, coupled with the desire to get out and push or do something, which lasted until my watch showed the hopelessness of the case, when it settled to a kind of dull despair.

San Toy was followed by *The Greek Slave*,

The Prefect Pomponius, in "The Greek Slave."

written by our old author Owen Hall, and containing
to my mind some of the finest music that Sydney
Jones has given us; notably the finale to Act I,
which is as strong as anything I can remember.
Here again the author's well-planned scheme suffered
under the necessity for introducing a totally fresh
and prominent character (for which he had naturally
made no allowance), for the reason that there was
an artist who, in the opinion of George Edwardes,
was to create a great sensation. This proceeding was
no doubt commercially sound, but it very much
upset the construction of the play and absolutely
necessitated a complete shuffling of the principal
parts.

This was the last piece in which I had the great
pleasure of being associated with Letty Lind, the
possessor of that marvellous gift of personality
which appeals so strongly to an audience. Her chief
attraction lay, of course, in her dancing, but she
had a sympathetic though very small voice, and,
while thoroughly understanding how to get the full
value of the points of her songs, had also the power
to give a pathetic touch to an occasional line which
was invaluable. I have never forgotten one such
line in the *Artist's Model*, where she was disguised as
a boy, and the students in mischief threaten to un-
clothe her and make her their model. They get as far
as laying rough hands on her, when she confesses her
sex in the simple words, "Please, I'm a little girl,"
and the mingled terror and shame in her voice

will, I am sure, be remembered by many besides myself.

My topical effort in this play was "1 Want to be Popular," and was very successful; indeed, I often hear it whistled now by strangers in the street who fancy, perhaps, they recognize the Prefect Pomponius.

Marie Tempest had a fine part in *Maia*, and she and Hayden Coffin were really great in the finale to which I have referred, the only mistake about which, in my opinion, was that it was really the end of the play, there being a truly dramatic moment when the girl finds her slave lover has been taken away, leaving only a statue in his place, and falls flat on the stage, dead, as I should have had it, but only fainting, in view of the second act. Marie Tempest was truly magnificent in this situation.

All kinds of wild rumours were rife concerning the authorship of the play to follow *The Greek Slave*, and eventually I believe at least two people established their claims to certain rights in *The Country Girl*, one of them by the aid of a lawsuit; but the only author we ever saw at rehearsal was Tanner, whose work for the stage speaks for itself and is quite capable of standing alone.

Huntley Wright's part was a great effort to break away from the Chinamen to which he had seemed to be condemned for so long, and it was certainly a relief to see him as a dapper little officer's servant, displaying the usual familiarity and intimacy with his master which is so marked a peculiarity of the stage sailor, as witness another part of the same kind in *The Dairy Maids*, where an able seaman seems to be escorted everywhere by an officer for whom he appears to have little respect and less terror. Hayden Coffin always lent himself very kindly to this situation, and it was a common thing at rehearsal to see him in a corner with Huntley Wright, who would illustrate certain bits of business he wished to put in, and which they would perfect thus in private. The second act scene was rather overwhelming, consisting chiefly of an enormous staircase coming down in two sweeps either side of the stage, almost to the prompt entrance, and Fred Kaye, gazing at it when first set up, said, "This piece ought to be called 'Act I—Our Farm,' 'Act II—Our Stairs.'" They appeared to be put there mainly for Huntley Wright to run up and down, and had nothing to do with the plot, though what the plot was it was impossible to tell after the piece had been going about a fortnight. I know that on the first night I, as Mr. Raikes, a supposedly "lost-years-ago" Englishman, turned up, having in some mysterious manner landed from a ship in Devonshire on a visit to my native land, bringing with me a little Princess whom, as Rajah of Bhong, I was very anxious to marry, but hesitated about owing to a fear of meeting the first (and genuine) Mrs. Raikes. Of course she was a guest at a house in the neighbourhood, and we met and complications ensued, but in less than a fortnight she ceased to be Mrs. Raikes and reappeared as Lady

Anchester, and a great part of the plot vanished with her; but this never seemed to make any difference to the Daly plays.

As a general rule I have a strong objection to seeing men in women's clothes on the stage, but in this play I was much amused by Huntley Wright disguised as an old scandal-monger, who sang a capital song about "Mrs. Brown," written by Paul Rubens. This is one of the few occasions I have seen this disguise adopted without any feeling of offence being engendered. He also had the good fortune of being closely associated in his comic scenes with Ethel Irving, and the two were extremely funny in a sketching scene in the first act. Maggie May was a great attraction in the piece, her song, "Under the Deodar," being perhaps the most popular number of all, though closely run by "Coo," which was sung by poor Lilian Eldee, who died not very long since.

Maggie May was another artist who possessed the gift of a personality appealing to the audience, and the fullness and resonance of her voice were a constant surprise, coming from so small a person, but she doubtless derived this from her Welsh ancestors. She did not remain in the cast for very long, and there was a succession of Princesses, more or less effective, but none who quite replaced her. Evie Greene also left us during the run, and her place was taken by Olive Morrell, who made a very striking figure in the ballroom scene, but was a little lacking in the vivacity which is so strongly marked with Evie

Photograph : A. Bassano.

THE RAJAH OF BHONG, IN "THE COUNTRY GIRL"

Greene. "Peace in the Valley of Bhong" was the title of my now inevitable topical song, and I should be afraid to say how many verses I wrote for it. There was a *cause célèbre* in the Divorce Court just then, which afforded me an excellent opportunity for a verse which even pleased me—a rather rare occurrence; and it was very amusing to find both parties to the suit, and others involved, making frequent appearances in the boxes and stalls to hear it. I also had a verse which was none too complimentary to Russia, at the time when there were certain complications threatened over the North Sea fishing-fleet affair, and on several occasions I had a whisper from a little bird that "the Russian Ambassador is in front." When the cue came for my song, I would notice him preparing to give great attention to this verse when it came, but, oddly enough, I invariably forgot to sing it when he was present. I have once or twice had a request from the Lord Chamberlain's office to relinquish singing a certain verse, but these have invariably been for a political reason, I am glad to say, and not because they were errors of taste. I used to get the most impossible kind of verses sent me by strangers, written mostly with an utter disregard of the air, and more often than not with too many feet in one line and not enough in the next. Owing to the elasticity of George Edwardes's contracts with his authors and composers he was able to introduce songs by other people, and being anxious to secure a number for Maggie May, I suggested to him a duet of my own on the old lines of Pierrette and Pierrot; the music was " arranged " by some one from my own tune, and the number used to go very well—in fact, so well, that it was very shortly cut. Some one did not like it.

XI

KINGSLEY's *Water-babies* had for many years dwelt in my mind as affording great possibilities for a children's play, and at odd times I had worked upon an adaptation of the book for this purpose, and during the run of the plays at Daly's I used to occupy my waits with perfecting the scenario, and writing the additional songs which I thought would be required. It was eventually completed, and in the spring of 1902 I read it to Mr. and Mrs. Bourchier, who were charmed with the idea. Bourchier immediately agreed to produce it at the Garrick, and made some suggestions as to the introduction of one or two scenes which I had left out, owing partly to a fear of overcrowding, and partly on account of the difficulties of scenery; which latter, Bourchier pointed out, were really non-existent. It was truly a labour of love rehearsing this play, and I did it entirely myself, with the exception of the dances, and Arthur Bourchier was so pleased with the result of my efforts that he kindly associated his name with mine as the producers. We had a great argument as to the Fairy Queen speaking Irish, for the reason that she appeared in the first act as The Irishwoman, but I

disliked it very much, and although he was very
obstinate about it he had to give way when I quoted
Kingsley to him : " You are no Irishwoman, by your
speech." Nellie Bowman made a splendid Tom,
and in her scenes with the master sweep Grimes,
excellently played by Darleigh, fairly brought her
audience to tears. Frederic Rosse composed most
of the music, and could well have done it all but
that, for some occult reason, a second composer was
introduced by the management. Alfred Cellier's
music to the song " I once had a dear little doll "
was of course used. The Lobster was very popular
with the little ones in the audience, and there
were great rejoicings when he fought and killed
the Otter in the lobster pot. On the first performance I was watching a sweet little girl in the stalls
who was much interested, and when the Lobster,
after the fight, announced his intention of having
a sleep because he had a " water-headache," she
turned to her mother, clapped her hands with delight, and shouted out, " Mummy—a water-headache
—how funny !" and I heard her talking of it as they
went out. I painted small panels in oils as models
of the scenes I wanted, and " Shiny Wall " came
out most effectively. The son of my old friend
Santley appeared as the Frozen Sailor in this scene,
and made good use of a capital voice. My greatest
delight was to sit in a box from which I could see
well over the house, and watch the enjoyment of the
children in front, which was, I really believe, equalled

by the pleasure taken in their work by those on the stage. Another old young friend of mine was the principal Water-baby, Miss Mary Collette, daughter of the mercurial Charles, and very sweet she looked. She married shortly after the run of the piece, and I always insisted that her appearance as a baby secured her a husband.

I had an awkward moment at one performance when sitting next a little girl I knew; poor Tom was being beaten by Grimes, and from tearfulness the little girl passed to indignation, and turning to me said, " Where's his father?" Now in Kingsley's book it is expressly stated that poor little Tom never knew his father, but I felt that this would not satisfy the child, who repeated her question imperiously; it then occurred to me to say he was dead, and this pacified her at once and she immediately asked for chocolates. I cannot quite follow the sequence of ideas, but so it happened, and I leave the solution to others.

Madge Titheradge was our *première danseuse* and made a great success with her dance outside the little school-house, or rather cottage; she danced with such evident enjoyment of her work. After seeing her in this and another play of mine I lost sight of her for some years, and going one night to the Play-house I was much pleased with the acting of a young girl in *The Drums of Oude*, and there was something about her which seemed familiar and yet I could not place her. On looking at the programme

I discovered her to be my little dancer, and was pleased to see that her early dancing had taught her to make strides in her profession.

This was followed at Christmas, 1904, by another play for children, which I had elaborated from two of the well-known " Dumpy books " called *Little Black Sambo* and *Little White Barbara*, for which I wrote two at least of what I venture to consider my best songs, but on this occasion the music was not done justice to, and owing to a misunderstanding I had with Bourchier I did not rehearse the piece myself and it suffered accordingly. Wilfred Bendall had written some charming and suitable music, but, without consulting me on the matter, some of the lyrics were given to other people to reset, and in addition to this slight, at the only rehearsal I attended the conductor informed me that he had " filled out " Bendall's score, the said score being made " light " at my request. Two of the best songs in the piece were in a part requiring a praetised singer, and my dismay at the engagement of Frank Lawton, the well-known whistler, for the part, may be better imagined than described. Admirable artist and superb whistler he undoubtedly is, but, as he himself admitted to me, he does not profess to sing.

Naturally I remonstrated with Bourchier on the subject, but to no effect, and it was one of those heart-breaking experiences which struggling authors have to put up with, as in spite of a written guarantee that "the songs should be sung," they were not given to any one else, and were mutilated to the extent of one verse only in each, being "given" by Mr. Lawton. This high-handed manner of ignoring an author's wishes would, in the case of some managers, be deemed absolute discourtesy and in others perhaps as demonstrating an appalling want of appreciation of the fact that the songs in a musical piece are intended to be heard. Either alternative is equally unpleasant to contemplate in the case of a man of Arthur Bourchier's well-known urbanity and intelligence (he is undoubtedly in some parts quite a good actor), so I prefer to think that other reasons existed for conduct which certainly imperilled the success of the play.

To turn to a more pleasing feature in connection with this piece, the engagement of little Iris Hawkins for Little White Barbara was nothing less than an inspiration on his part, and contributed very largely to what success was achieved by the piece; there were other clever people in it, notably a sweet little girl who played the Chinese Dolly, Nellie Bowman as Black Sambo, and Frank Lacy as Jake. Of course Frank Lawton's whistling was a great feature, but should have been a special turn, with the songs rendered by some one else. I attended the first performance, and was gratified to find the play go as well as it did, though it afforded abundant evidence of the lack of assistance on the part of some one with a knowledge of musical requirements, and

I wrote a letter suggesting certain alterations. I saw the play once or perhaps twice more, and some of these had been adopted and others ignored, so I went no more, having surrendered all hope of seeing it in correct form until it returns to me in the fullness of time. I do not wish it thought that I am holding a brief for authors, not having the status which would warrant such a procedure; it is merely a statement of my feelings concerning an important experience in my life.

In March, 1904, was produced at Daly's that most attractive play *The Cingalee*, remarkable for its local colour and the absence of much of the go-as-you-please work so prevalent in the modern musical play, that is to say on its production, for it was not very long before "additional numbers" were introduced at the expense of certain picturesque items that were not considered bright enough. The first night of *The Cingalee* was nearly as remarkable in its way as that of *The Mikado*, in fact, the nearest approach to it in enthusiasm that I have known. For some reason which I could not fathom, George Edwardes was not pleased with the way it was constructed, and chopping and changing began almost immediately. One number for four ladies and their cavaliers, which had taken weeks to perfect, disappeared bodily, while others were twisted round, cut shorter, and put into different places, until the play differed so much from the original that it was hardly recognizable; however, it ran for a whole year, thus proving Edwardes's judgment correct, although there was nothing to show that it would not have done so if left alone.

This is the only piece I remember Fred Kaye having a song in; it was called "Freddy was fond of fireworks," but I fancy it did not even survive till the first night. Some one who saw the dress rehearsal and noticed the long cane I carried very kindly sent me a note pointing out that it was not the correct thing at all, and with the note came a cane that had actually been the property of a Cingalese nobleman, a most welcome present and one that I treasure. Isabel Jay made her entrance in a rickshaw, right from the back of the stage to the footlights, and at one rehearsal had an accident that might have been serious, the man in the shafts tripping over something and letting the machine go over backwards; most fortunately it was on the slope instead of the level stage, but Miss Jay thought it bad enough. Coffin was our hero, as usual, and Isabel Jay, his cousin, had come out to the tea plantation to marry him, but found him in love with one of the tea-girls, betrothed to myself, Boobhamba; when Bradfield was brought into the piece it was arranged that he and Miss Jay should be a kind of second pair of lovers, and she was to take no interest in Coffin, so why she came out there at all was a mystery if one stopped to think. This was the play in which Ida˘ Renè was to have appeared, and, in fact, she rehearsed till within three or four days of the production, when she came to the conclusion that the part was not suited to her, and so left us somewhat suddenly; fortunately, that clever little artist Gracie Leigh was at hand to take up the part and play it successfully, at such short notice, not that her success was surprising, as in addition to her talent she possesses that personality which appeals so trongly to an audience, and is so rare a gift, especially in the sterner sex.

Once again fate played me a sorry trick in leaving me voiceless on a first night, as in *Patience* some years before, but on this occasion it hardly mattered so much, as Boobhamba was not all - important to the piece; indeed, as one critic wrote, with such undue prominence given to one or two rôles it was a waste of good artists in the others. Adrian Ross had great trouble in finding me a good topical song for this play, and on the first night I was glad to escape by whispering one verse of the one I had, which was never used again. This was partly on account of my loss of voice, but also because of the lateness of the hour. The first act took very nearly two hours to play, and there was then a long wait before the second was ready. The audience had begun to show signs of impatience at the length of the first act, and I think were so relieved when it did finish as to feel no resentment at the wait, which they filled up by singing the National Anthem and cheering Her Majesty the Queen, who, with Princess Victoria, was occupying the Royal box.

Adrian Ross came to talk over the topical song with me the next evening (I had promptly cut the one of the night before), and we had a long discussion as to "refrains," but do as we might we could not fix on a good catch-word; he was leaving me, in despair of finding one, when in answer to some remark of mine he replied, "Well—there isn't much more to say."—"There it is!" I shouted.— "What?" he replied.—"Why the catch-word for the new song," I said. "Write it down before you forget it, and let me have the first verse to-morrow." He went away quite happy, and in about a week the song was put in and turned out quite a good one.

I think Lionel Monckton did some of his best work in the music for this play, and I should much like to see him entrusted with a libretto containing a coherent plot and witty dialogue, and free from the "introduced numbers" that so often upset the sequence of things. I think it was at my instance that he wrote an unaccompanied (or very nearly so) quartette for the piece, and very graceful and charming it was, quite in the best traditional Savoy style, but the voices did not seem to blend as they should have done, and although successful it did not gain the applause that I think it deserved.

There was an idea of effecting an extra amount of realism by the introduction in the first act of some elephants, and absurd as it may seem it was quite seriously considered, as I found one day when having lunch with George Edwardes, during an interval of rehearsing, at the "Cavour." A well-known agent came to him during lunch and said, "I have got those elephants for you to look at, Mr. Edwardes."— "Oh!" said George. "Well, send 'em up to rehearsal to-morrow, will you?" The man looked a little doubtful, and George said, "By the way—what do they want for them?" The price was named and that settled the elephant question, and to make up for the loss of such an attraction the agent was invited to find something exceptional in the way of dancers, which he did in the shape of a troupe called "the Three Amaranths," who did some marvellous gyrations of a dancing kind, the smallest of the three, a mere child, concluding the "turn" with what looked like a horribly dangerous mode of throwing herself about. This took place in what was called the Parahara, which appeared to the uninitiated to be some kind of festival commencing with priests and prayers, and ending with dancing and devilry, which, I imagine, is a mixture not entirely confined to the Cingalese.

There was a great run on animal duets about this time, and a very clever monkey duet, given by Gracie Leigh and Huntley Wright, was much liked, in fact, one of the critics alluded to it as "the *clou* of the performance." As this was one of the "introduced numbers" this criticism may appear unfair to the author and composer of all else, but after all it was only the expression of one opinion. It was replaced later by The Gollywogs, an effort to get away from bird and animal life, and a very successful one at that, becoming so popular as to necessitate gollywogs being given away to all the children visitors to the theatre at Christmas.

XII

FINDING myself one of the unemployed owing to the sweeping changes George Edwardes thought it his policy to make when casting the *Little Michus*, it occurred to me that I could not do better than follow the example set by so many of my colleagues of the stage and try my hand at music-hall work. No sooner thought than done. After an interview with the courteous Mr. George Ashton, who represented to Mr. Oswald Stoll that "now was his opportunity," he seemed to think it was ; and I signed a contract for eight weeks, with option of a further eight, with a certain amount of trepidation at the novelty of giving a " turn " by myself. I wrote a song which I called *The Moody Mariner*, intending to sing a couple of verses, then tell a story, and wind up with a final verse. The story I chose was one of Jacobs's most humorous efforts, in my estimation (about the sea serpent), which is to be found in his book *Many Cargoes*, and which I had frequently told with great success at concerts and suppers ; somewhat abridged, of course, but with none of the fun left out. Walter Slaughter wrote the music of the song for me, and the management provided a delightful scene. The "turn" was to finish with a sentimental ballad (also by myself and Slaughter), about a sailor and his lass, called "Across the Silent Way," the last verse being sung with the lights down, and a vision of the lovers on the shore, where they were supposed to "walk," thrown on the back cloth. Both the songs invariably went well, but for some reason or other the galleryites would not have the recitation. I fancy it was too long, but anyhow, on my first essay, they began to murmur, then said something I failed to catch ; but I grasped the situation correctly, for when I said to Slaughter, "I think I'd better sing," there was a round of applause. This of course happened at the matinée, and the trouble was how to fill out the time for that evening, for I determined not to risk it again.

My old friend "topical verse" came to the rescue, and by night-time I had written two, both of which were successful, and the situation was saved.

This "turn" lasted the whole eight weeks, with of course a constant change of verse, and it was in this song that I created a record for myself. The final tie of the Association Football Cup was being played at the Crystal Palace, and I determined to sing them a verse giving the score at half-time, hoping to know it before I went on. I had written the verse and had an alternative two lines to suit whichever team had scored, but when the curtain rose for my turn the news had not come. While I was singing the

K

song I saw the stage manager in the wings waving a telegram. After finishing the verse I went to the wings, got the envelope, opened it before the audience, and sang them the information that Aston Villa was a goal ahead at half-time. I do not think I have ever had a greater success with a verse.

I was greatly indebted for my success to the efforts of the choir, which in those days filled the boxes just outside the proscenium, and apart from singing glees (often encored) were invaluable in the refrains of my two songs. It must have been an awful strain to them, being present at four performances a day, not to speak of rehearsals at odd times between, but I am sorry to see they have disappeared.

Meanwhile I had been busily engaged preparing another sketch in case it should be wanted, and towards the end of the eight weeks I had word from Stoll that he would like a change if I could manage it; so we began to rehearse *The Tramp*, to which Walter Slaughter had also put music. There was a quite beautiful little introduction sung by the choir to take up the curtain, and then a cart and horse came on, the real thing too (it seemed wonderful to me), with some children in the cart and others walking, and the tramp, who was an old soldier, helping himself along by holding on to the tail-board, which he let go, to sink on an old stump and rest. The children gathered round him, and a rough boy dragged his sister away and sneered at the old fellow

Photograph · Alfred Ellis & Walery.

THE TRAMP. (SONG SCENA.)

for "a tramp." He then sang about his soldiering and finally fell dead. This was by way of being a new departure for me, but it proved popular enough to run for the remaining eight weeks of my engagement. The rehearsals for all the items used to take place on Sundays; there was no other possible day on which to try scenery and dresses, and I remember that on the day we had the final rehearsal of *The Tramp*, the choir and all the extra people had been called at ten in the morning, and when we left (I was last) it was past eleven at night, and then there remained a few odd jobs to attend to on Monday morning before the first performance, which was known to the artists as "the Dust-bin," and not very popular.

The revolving stage was of great assistance in setting the scenes, two or three being in readiness, and only requiring the lowering of a sky-border or ceiling when turned to the auditorium. The first time I came down and found my scene set like this, right at the back, I thought I would wait and travel round with it, which I did, but the sensation was so peculiar that on the rise of the curtain I forgot my words and felt very awkward for a time.

One night I was informed on arrival that the heavy curtain, which was worked by hydraulic power, had refused to act, the water-main had burst somewhere in Piccadilly, and it affected several theatres. I was told that I should have to walk off after I had finished my sketch, which was rather awkward, as I was supposed to fall dead. All they could do to help me was to turn all lights down completely, and even then two of the stage hands must have thought I had failed to understand the position, as they came on and helped me up, one of them saying, " You've got to get up and go off, guv'nor." There was a laugh, but not so great a one as I feared.

The programme occasionally got overcrowded as to length, and there was tremendous trouble in getting some of the artists to curtail their " turns," and one night, to my dismay, the stage manager came to me on my arrival with " Mr. Stoll's compliments, and could you oblige him by singing one verse of your song?" This mutilation struck me as so extraordinary and also useless that I said I would much rather cut the whole number. However, this, according to the stage manager, Mr. Stoll objected to. I went to the front of the house to interview him if possible, but in vain, and came back to announce my determination to sing two verses and no less (leaving out one). As I crossed the stage to go to my room, to my dismay I heard the band play the opening music of my scene! How I did it I hardly know, but I dressed, made up (badly), and got on in time. I afterwards heard that Mr. Stoll's request had been distorted on the way, and he had asked me to " leave out " one verse, a very different affair, and when I saw him he was much annoyed at the trouble the misstatement had caused me.

There was a very zealous and inventive stage manager there who gave, as a rule, invaluable assistance to the artist, but he nearly spoilt my Tramp scene by the introduction of too many lantern-slide effects, depicting the war scene the old man was singing about, and I was so curious to see them myself that the second time they were used I turned half round all the time, and this did not add to the intelligibility of the song.

During my stay here I wrote a little kind of "Rip-van-Winkle" sketch for Courtice Pounds, who made a great success with it, and the inventive manager aforesaid introduced a capital dance for Pounds and a crowd of little children, which was most effective. Among other turns Mrs. Brown Potter appeared in a condensed version of *Pagliacci*, which was wonderfully well put on, but failed to become very popular for some reason.

Before my sixteen weeks were up I had signed with Frank Curzon to appear in *The White Chrysanthemum* at the Criterion, Mr. Stoll very kindly waiving his option to send me round the country or renew for London, but at his request I went for a special week to Manchester, where I had a most disappointing experience. I played both *The Moody Mariner* and *The Tramp* on different evenings during the week, and they did not seem to care an atom about either of them. I was rather surprised, as one expects anything with the London seal of success on it to go at least fairly well in the provinces. It was a depressing week, and I was glad to get back to London for rehearsals.

This engagement at the Coliseum was not my first appearance on "the halls," as I have played for benefits at the Alhambra, the Empire, and the Palace. The latter was on the occasion of some kind of birthday compliment to Mr. Morton, the father of music halls, and I determined to make a fresh departure in my contribution. I therefore elected to sing a coon song of my own, and "black" for it. Daly's Theatre being so handy I thought 1 would make use of my own room and just run over when ready, but I was met at the stage door by a small crowd of little children, who followed me all the way to the Palace stage door, waited, and escorted me back again, all the while making personal remarks of a not too complimentary nature, much to the amusement of the passers-by who noticed the little comedy.

It was some consolation to find the critic of the *Daily Telegraph* the next day saying in his notice of the performance that it was a treat to find me giving them a change from the unvarying song or recitation so usual among artists appearing at benefits.

The contrast between the stage at the Coliseum and that of the Criterion, which was the scene of my next engagement, is rather marked, and for the first few rehearsals I felt as if I dared hardly move for fear of knocking against somebody or something.

This sensation, of course, soon wore off, though I must say I prefer a somewhat larger stage than we had for *The White Chrysanthemum*, a very pretty little play and an effort in the direction of comedy with music, which I think deserved a more lasting success than it achieved. Some of Howard Talbot's melodies were quite delightful, and naturally received full justice at the hands of Isabel Jay and Henry Lytton. I thoroughly enjoyed my part of the Admiral, and was fortunate with my topical song, which happened to be an easy one to write verses for, and effective in its stage setting too, with a chorus of bluejackets headed by a bos'n. This was the first time I had the pleasure of acting with Millie Legarde, an excellent exponent of the best style of light comedy, and quick to respond to any interpolations in either words or business. The piece opened very prettily with Isabel Jay discovered in a hammock, waited on by a little Jap girl, and is one of the few instances I remember where the *prima donna* was content without the orthodox "entrance" usually so well led up to. After her experience of rickshaws at Daly's it was no wonder that Miss Jay was nervous in attempting it again here, but possibly the very short distance to be traversed made all the difference, and there never was the slightest approach to an accident. Millie Legarde always declared that I left her very little room in the one we occupied together, and I feel sure that no one can blame me when I admit that she spoke the truth. Curzon

came to me one night with the news that he had
been asked by some one in authority to suppress one
of my verses, and he seemed rather upset over it
until I assured him it had happened before. As it
was not political I took some pains to find out the
reason of this *clôture*, and discovered that the personal vanity of the private individual lampooned had
received such a shock as to necessitate an "application to restrain." I felt very much tempted to put
the verse back again, and so did Curzon when I told
him what I knew.

It was quite thought at the time that in Leedham
Bantock and Arthur Anderson two authors had been
discovered who were really going to improve the
status of musical comedy, and possibly if they had
been able to keep their company together, play in
the same theatre, and produce as good work as *The
White Chrysanthemum* it might have been so, but
their next joint effort was none too successful, and I
believe the partnership is now dissolved. Our uni-
forms of white drill were most effective, if perhaps
slightly incorrect, but so slightly as only to be
noticed by the expert naval officer, although this
is really a very important point, members of either
service being very particular in this respect ; indeed, I
once heard a criticism of a play in which some
officers of a definite regiment were represented, from
the lips of a genuine member of the regiment, to
this effect, "I think it's a rotten piece ! Why, the
fellows have got the wrong buttons on their tunics !"

The end of the run of *Chrysanthemum* found me once again unemployed, and I unfortunately met in Regent Street one day a concert-tour agent who had been associated with me once before, proving himself a genuine hard worker, and he suggested that "now was the time for a short tour." Well, I thought perhaps it might be, so we set to work fixing dates and a programme. Nothing could have been more satisfactory than both turned out, but the results were not commensurate. My company consisted only of Harold Grimston and his charming wife, who sings under the name of Robertson, he being an accompanist and also a pianist of such class as to receive encores for his two solos, which I had always great trouble to make him accept. It is a somewhat rare thing for a pianist whose hair is only of normal length to be really successful. We went to some twelve or fourteen little towns and thoroughly enjoyed the experience, even though it was (to me) rather costly. One day's work was pretty heavy. We gave a matinée at Folkestone and then travelled to Deal to give an evening recital, and the margin on arrival was only about twenty minutes. I insisted on going to Market Harborough for a night, having once driven through the little town and been struck with its restful appearance. We did fairly well, but were told here (as in most other places) that we ought to have come a month earlier. I find this is nearly always the case with concert parties. I cannot help thinking that the sea-coast towns and provinces generally have been overdone with concerts and recitals, for I have seen some appalling figures in the way of "returns" to companies carrying some six or eight people of note. The fact is that there is little room nowadays for anything between Paderewski and Pierrots, and the outlook is not improved by the larger hotels in the seaside resorts giving their patrons a free concert after dinner, with at least one good artist to listen to. People are hardly likely to turn out and walk perhaps some little distance and pay for seats unless the attraction is really great, when they can do so well where they are. But we finished up at the Hampstead Conservatoire, and during the evening I was "approached" for a part in Charles Wyndham's revival of *The Candidate* at Wyndham's Theatre. Being "approached" always strikes me as such a quaint (if not silly) way of expressing a business transaction, and yet I do not quite see how else to put it. I was amenable to the approachment, and it led to one of the most delightful engagements of my career, though all too short. Wyndham, of course, I had known for years, but it was the first occasion I had ever been associated with him, and I do not mean it to be the last, if constant reminders to that effect are of any use. We were a happy little company, and I think Wyndham thoroughly enjoyed the short lapse into farce, and found it a relief from the high-minded, virtuous kind of person he has been playing so much of late. He was much amused at one or two gags

I introduced, and on my telling him one night that I was going to sing at a certain exit said he would come and listen. I sang a bar or two of " Under the Deodar " with great success, but I do not think he heard me, as I received neither a compliment nor my notice.

XIII

JUST as I was beginning to feel quite comfortable with a part in which I had no music to consider, the run of *The Candidate* came to an end, and I was once more a homeless wanderer. I had heard rumours of the revival of *The Geisha*, and rather flattered myself that I might be asked to take up my old part; however, no such invitation arrived, and I eventually promised to play in a new opera by yet another couple of fresh aspirants to fame and fortune in the persons of Michael Faraday and Frederick Fenn, the latter of whom was already known as the author of certain plays without music. This opera was called *Amāsis*, and when I was given the book to read, in order to judge whether the part suggested for me was suitable, I had a vague impression that I had already had it submitted to my judgment, which turned out to be the fact. My original idea about it was that it would be handicapped by the costumes, which gave so little opportunity for any display of grace or elegance among the women concerned, and that the lyrics were somewhat laboured, and though excellent to read would not be so effective when sung. Both these views were to some extent endorsed on the production of the piece, but there was more to go through before this much-desired event happened.

In the first place I heard that the management at Daly's were not altogether satisfied with the cast of *The Geisha*, and that the comedian who was appearing in my part was finding it somewhat irksome to follow the lines laid down, not only by tradition, but also by the exigencies of the piece. These rumours culminated in George Edwardes asking me to return to the fold and take up my old part, while his other comedian took a well-earned rest. This was naturally a great compliment to me, but I should have appreciated it more fully (as also, I venture to think, would have the revival) had it been offered to me before the piece was produced. However, I went, and was received with open arms by those of my old colleagues still at Daly's. Great pressure was brought to bear upon me to resign the *Amāsis* engagement and stay on, and in my endeavour to do so I got as far as an interview with the managing director of Amāsis Limited (a syndicate to exploit it had been formed), at which I asked him to let me off, though I had not signed anything and was not legally bound; but when he asked me point-blank whether I did not consider myself morally bound to them, I was obliged to confess that I did, and that I had come to him feeling rather ashamed of my request. This terminated the discussion, conducted with an urbanity on his side which was a striking tribute to his diplomacy and good taste, and I left him prepared to exchange the position of a Japanese nobleman I was playing for the higher one of Pharaoh when desired.

In this connection I hope I may be excused in quoting what I felt to be a very great compliment paid to me in the *Evening Standard*, which said, in announcing my return to Daly's, " This is a distinct triumph for one of the ablest of the comedians of the old legitimate school as distinct from the new generation of individualistic entertainers, who are certainly vastly amusing, but who are not actors in the strictly artistic sense of the word—that is to say, their humour provokes laughter because of the personality of the player and of his funniments, which, amusing as they are, are quite 'outside the picture' and have no regard to the unities, locality, or period of the piece."

The Geisha revival lasted only a little longer than that of the *Gaiety Girl*, all these pieces undoubtedly lacking the qualities which distinguish the Gilbert-Sullivan creations, most of the dialogue and the whole of the music of which seems to have been written for all time.

The rehearsals of *Amasis* were in full swing, and having capitulated I attended the next one to which I was called, and was agreeably surprised on hearing some of the music. Louis Calvert, the managing director to whom I have before alluded, was superintending the rehearsals, with a capable lieutenant in

As Pharaoh in "Amāsis."

Frank Stanhope and occasional suggestions from a
modest individual whom I eventually found to be
the author, Frederick Fenn. Calvert's treatment of
the piece was (naturally to so excellent an actor)
based entirely on strong dramatic lines, invaluable
no doubt for a play, but wanting somewhat in the
lightness necessary to comic opera. To do him justice I must admit that he had the courage of his
convictions, and any views in opposition to his own
were very definitely pronounced to be incorrect; this
led at one rehearsal to such a difference of opinion
between himself and the musical director, as to cul-
minate in the latter leaving the theatre in dudgeon.
I found the construction of the piece vastly different
from what it was when I first read it, some time before, but later on it came back almost entirely to its
original shape, much to the gratification of the
author. One important alteration was the elimination of Pharaoh (the part I played) from the first
act; this, I argued from the beginning, was unwise;
but it was persisted in until the critics, with hardly a
dissentient voice, strongly recommended the alternative, and after some weeks the change was effected.
I also advocated the insertion of a topical song in
the part, the objector in this case being the composer, who expressed a wish to depart from the
beaten track of modern musical pieces; but he eventually gave way gracefully, and the song was not the
least successful number, although it must be admitted on his side of the argument that one critic

expressed regret at its introduction. On the other hand, one important journal said that all through the first act they were anticipating my arrival with a song in which "mummies and motor-buses, pyramids and Poplar would be jumbled up in a delicious song." Ruth Vincent had a part which gave her capital opportunities for the display of her admirable vocalization without unduly straining her powers of acting, and the soubrette part was well played by her sister Madge. Whitworth Mitton was a kind of ragged rival to the gorgeous Prince Anotep, played in vigorous fashion by Roland Cunningham, but Mitton was severely handicapped by a fearful costume and wig which robbed the part of much of the romance and the sympathy it should have claimed. It was also intended that he should wear a hump on his back, but the very idea of such disfigurement gave him one, and he declined to make use of the false presentment; it was, however, carefully preserved, carried all round the provinces when we went touring with the play, and eventually given to him on the last week of the tour, as a birthday present.

Although I had known Norman Salmond for many years, this was the first occasion I had ever worked with him, and he did yeoman service as the High Priest, his carriage and stature making a most striking figure among us. The dramatic possibilities of the opera were so strongly insisted upon by Calvert at rehearsal that the company began to wonder if it were really a light opera or not, and as Calvert himself began to see that musical numbers called for a different kind of treatment, it was eventually agreed that the later rehearsals should be subject to suggestions from me. My first step was to introduce a kind of dance for Norman Salmond and his satellites, and Calvert's horror at "the High Priest dancing" was too great for words; but it secured an encore for the number on the first night, as Norman, waltzing round the stage, using his staff of office as a fairy wand, was a sight for the gods, who want amusing as much as mortals. We set to work very shortly after the production to bring the piece more into line with opera than drama. I was brought into the first act, and had an additional song in the second, which I wrote myself, called "Lovely Woman," and more fun being imported in both acts, the result was quite happy, and in spite of an unusually hot August and September we played to wonderful business.

A great factor in this added success was the importation of a little comedian named Lauri de Frece, who has a method decidedly original and unforced, though with the tendency of most comedians to over-elaborate occasionally; however, you cannot put old heads on young shoulders, and it takes experience to learn how to let well alone. His part of Sebak, the keeper of the Crocodiles, was an infinitesimal one at first start, but in his hands it grew to be quite one of the most important without being unduly so. The contrast between my bulk and his extremely slight figure was very useful in some of the comedy scenes, as such contrast invariably is, and both of us being fairly ready in replying to any unexpected speech on the part of the other, these scenes were worked up to become quite a feature of the piece. We were asked one night to "fill out a few minutes" for some reason which I forget, and we did it so successfully that it was difficult to get back to "the author," much to the delight of all the chorus. The part of Ptolemy, which was originally played by Herbert Ross (his second appearance with me in musical comedy), was one of those disappointing kind of rôles, from the artist's point of view, which seem to offer great opportunities and yet which, however well played, amount to nothing out of the common. It was undertaken later on by Reginald White, who certainly extracted from it the most possible, once again vindicating the Savoy school, he having been with the repertoire company for some time.

We were obliged to vacate the New Theatre, owing to the return of Julia Neilson and Fred Terry with their hardy annual *The Scarlet Pimpernel*, and after a lengthy hesitation over the choice of three theatres at least, our management finally decided to squeeze us into the Criterion. The steps of the temple, as used in our first act, would have over-lapped the stage into Regent Street and the Hay-market, and everything else was in the same ratio, so there was a general reduction of everything to fit the smaller compass; and there we proceeded merrily until within a few weeks of the spring tour which had been arranged, and on which it was intended to take the entire London company. Eventually it was decided to leave out Ruth Vincent, and there was a hue and cry to discover a substitute for this popular soprano, not a very easy matter, as at present there seems a great dearth of good voices; however, Constance Drever was discovered almost at the last moment, and in her capable hands the part lost none of its significance. We commenced the tour at Stratford, London, where there is a fine theatre, and it was instructive to notice how, at this short distance only from the West End, certain of the "points" made were quite distinct from the original.

I developed a throat attack and could hardly last out the week, but being always regarded as a kind of cast-iron person, there was no understudy, and I just struggled through by dint of cutting one song after the other until on the Saturday there was no song left. At Kennington the following week my place was taken by the composer of the music, Faraday, who had never acted before, and attacked his task in so light-hearted a manner as to be even capable, on the second night, of introducing gags of his own. One of the company said to me some months later, " Next to you, Barry, he's the best Pharaoh we've had, but I think he'd better stick to composing."

On Sunday, September 22nd, 1907, I rejoined the company at King's Cross on a bitterly cold morning, where I found a very gorgeous " special," in which I had a little saloon all to myself like Royalty, waiting to take us to Hull, where we arrived after a very comfortable and fast journey. Norman Salmond, de Frece, Mitton, and myself stayed at the same hotel all through the trip, and were a very cheery party, with just enough occasional differences to afford the necessary vinegar in the salad.

This was my first appearance in Hull, and the whole week was a pleasant surprise to me, after the way in which I had heard the town and its audiences alluded to by certain, evidently unappreciated, members of the theatrical profession.

We golfed during the week at Brough, one of the best inland courses I know, and the home of several of Yorkshire's most noted players. We had lunch at a charming little inn called "The Ferry" (why I do not know, as there was no ferry within miles of it), which had a quaint motto over the bar.

> The Lord helps the man who helps himself,
> But the Lord help the man caught helping himself here.

I made my first appearance as a caddie one afternoon. There was a ladies' competition, and several of us carried for them instead of playing. One of the men of our party got lost on the links, and under the impression that he had found the club-house, went in at the side door of a private house and ordered beer ! He was received by the cook as a burglar, and left hurriedly.

Miss Drever seemed a little uncertain about her "cues" the first two nights here, and the stage manager suggested, when I spoke to him about it, that it was possibly the fault of Faraday, which seemed odd to me, as he was in London. My voice being still rather rough, I made up my mind to cut my topical song the second night, but the chorus was evidently determined I should not, gave the cue for it by coming on, and I had to sing it!

On my arrival at the theatre one night I found a representative of the *Daily Express* waiting for me with news of the death that day of my dear colleague, Rosina Brandram, and a request that I would write a short "appreciation" of her for the next day's edition. This was a phase of journalistic enterprise which I experienced for the first time; I dictated the article to the pressman while dressing and making up; it was wired to London before the curtain had been up five minutes, and the paper was lying on my breakfast table the next morning. Although I knew that dear old Rosie was ill, I had no idea it was so serious, and it made me feel very sad, but the footlights have a marvellous power of evoking a forgetfulness of everything but the matter in hand, and until the play was over I hardly realized that yet another link of the olden time was broken.

Roland Cunningham was unable to sing on the Saturday, and his understudy played at the matinée extremely well, but not so well at night. I have often noticed this effect in similar cases, and am inclined to believe that the nervousness of the initial effort is a great factor in the success.

Norman Salmond is a native of Hull, and we spent a most interesting morning going over his old crushing-mill, and the welcome given him by some of his old hands was a tribute worth the acceptance of any one. We thereupon dubbed him King of Yorkshire, and it was a great sight to see Norman with his long strides walking twenty yards ahead of the rest of us. We could never keep up with him after this in Hull, but I extracted a definite promise that in other towns he would modify his regal bearing and pace sufficiently to allow of our walking abreast.

There was a dense fog which accompanied us on Sunday the whole way from Hull to Sheffield, not only delaying our arrival, but completely hiding the glorious view of the town from the station; but it had disappeared on the Monday morning when we went for our usual exercise to Shireoaks, a very delightful course and by no means too easy. During a ten-minutes wait for our return train we went into the little village inn adjoining the station, to look at some stuffed fish, and on entering the sanded parlour found it occupied by some dozen colliers, taking a well-earned pint on the way home. I was much struck by the good manners displayed by these rough-looking men, who were grouped round the fire, some two or three of them rising on our entrance and inviting us to take their seats. Norman

Salmond promptly offered "drinks all round," and on the mugs of beer being brought I led off with "Come, landlord, fill the flowing bowl," and with Mitton, de Frece, and Salmond joining in the chorus we "let it rip" for all we were worth, intensely to the delight of our hearers, one old man saying he'd heard nothing like it for years, and he hoped we'd come again.

We were the guests that night of Colonel Vickers of Vickers and Maxim fame, who adds to his business ability the reputation of being a most delightful host, which he afforded us several opportunities of endorsing most cordially. There was some amusement caused at the menu of this particular supper, which certainly was rather odd : oysters, salmon mayonnaise, dressed crab, foie gras, and ices, for the peculiar nature of which Colonel Vickers declared I was to blame, having told him that for the time being I was on a fish diet ! However, we were none the worse for it on the following day, when a large party of us went over the big-gun manufactory, with the Colonel and Major Leslie as cicerone, and it was a wonderful experience to see a block of white-hot steel of about fifty tons weight being rolled into an armour plate, a very beautiful effect being secured by throwing on to the steel large armfuls of brushwood just as the plate went under the huge roller, the sparks from which, as it caught fire in one blaze, leapt fully twenty feet.

I had a pleasant trip to town by the breakfast

train one morning, having just an hour and a half for lunch at my home at Putney and being back at Sheffield at 6.30 to the tick, as timed by the Great Central. It was a "non-stop" return, the pleasure of the run being only marred by the presence of one of those railway bores who will insist on talking to everybody all the time and invariably about nothing.

The end of a cheery week saw us speeding northward to Edinburgh, with a return of the frost, and the snow lying all the way from York to our destination.

XIV

"Amasis" Tour

THE morning after our arrival in Edinburgh we went out to Barnton in pursuance of our strict regime of "exercise on Monday if no other day," and it was rather odd to find brilliant warm sunshine and snow underfoot. However, we played a round, though Norman Salmond expressed great displeasure at the course being played backwards, by way of resting the greens.

There was great fun in the selection of our bedrooms when the four of us arrived on the Sunday. It appeared that Mitton and Salmond had been somewhat cramped at the last town, and there was a great struggle to get first out of the lift, in which my dignity would not allow me to take part, and little de Frece had naturally no chance. Salmond was the first to "get a Ball down," as he styled selecting a room, Mitton being a good second, then de Frece. I strolled up last, having some idea that the manageress might have reserved me something, an idea which was well founded, and the result was an absolute palace of a room. Norman Salmond's conscience must have smitten him (he is one of the most conscientious artists I know), for he shouted from his room, " Barry, if you're not comfortable you can take mine." I replied, in as hurt a tone as I could manage, "Thanks very much, but I can put up with this; it doesn't matter." He forthwith came along to look at my room and was duly astonished, called to Mitton, and they both heartily enjoyed the way in which the laugh had turned against them.

I had another turn of laryngitis this week, and had to give up after the Monday; felt very much like the Prisoner of Chillon when they all left me to go to work on Tuesday night, and the feeling was evidently a sort of premonition, for while I sat playing patience a mouse jumped up on the table and stayed quite a long time while I fed it with crumbs of cake. It took a dislike to a cough lozenge I offered it, however, and left me, never to return.

We had a glorious drive to Luffness for a day's golf, which wound up with a blizzard. I was very badly beaten by Graham Walker, but Mitton made a great fight with A. M. Ross. I was thankful that our host, George Law, had a covered car, in which I slept like a dormouse all the way back to Edinburgh.

As I was not expected to appear that night I saw the opera from "the front," and came to the conclusion that it really was an exceptionally fine company and a capital piece. It being de Frece's birthday (his seventeenth, he told us, but if true he must have commenced to acquire worldly wisdom in the cradle), it was made an occasion of a festal supper, from which I retired early—that is, about three o'clock, having arranged with my old friend, W. W. Macfarlane, to go to Muirfield for the day, with Norman Salmond, Mitton, and de Frece, who had all gone to bed about 6.30. I succeeded in rousing the two former, but his birthday had been too much for de Frece. Our Saturday night performance was received with great enthusiasm, and the audience insisted on a speech from me—a novel experience.

A windy morning, with rain, snow, and sleet, greeted our departure from the capital of Bonnie Scotland, and on my walk to the station in my best rough-weather overcoat I was forced to take shelter in the niche of a bridge. While there my friends, the Laws, drove by on their way to see us off. George Law pointed me out, but the ladies declined to recognize me, asserting that it was not me, but a tramp. We had an amusing experience of the cinematograph here, being taken entering the train, leaving for Glasgow, arriving there, and disembarking—all of which was done at the Waverley Station. The author of the play travelled with me on this occasion, having much to discuss about the piece and being also solicitous as to my constantly recurring attacks of hoarseness, which involved such frequent absences, to the detriment of the ensemble. The journey was a short one, and there was no undue strain upon our friendly relations.

We had a great day at Prestwick during the week, being entertained at lunch by Mr. Hutchinson of

"Kite" fame; and for the afternoon match Robb, the amateur champion, gave the best ball of myself and Mitton a bad beating.

Glasgow is also memorable to me for a "first experience," which I sincerely trust may also prove a last, which was, that during the first act my voice completely gave out and I was unable to finish the evening's work. Fortunately there was a "week out" for all of us after this town, and Monday saw me, after consulting my doctor, sent home to bed with orders to write all communications on a slate! I began to wonder if I were going to be a spirit, but by dint of obeying "doctor's orders," I found myself well enough to leave for Newcastle after a week's rest, but broke down again after the first night, and did not appear again until the Thursday. The directors of Amāsis Limited were naturally much upset over my frequent relapses, and, guided by one of their number, took the rather strong step of "cancelling my contract" (which, of course, they could not do), and covering the bills announcing us the next week in Birmingham with the name of another artist, not unknown to fame as a dramatic actor, but with less singing voice when perfectly well than I had when perfectly ill!

The artist in question spent the greater part of the journey from Newcastle to Birmingham with the musical conductor, striking out "a few bars" here and there throughout the opera, entirely without reference to the singer concerned, with the result that on the first performance at the latter town, the tenor and the chorus came to utter grief in the difficult finale to Act I.

I left for town on the Monday, after making an offer to appear and do the best I could, which was refused in a spirit of confidence hardly justified by the result, as I received a telegram the next morning asking me to take up the part again the following week. This my doctor refused to allow me to do, and it was finally decided that I should rejoin for Manchester in a fortnight's time; and I was meanwhile kept amused by letters from my friends in the company detailing the humours of the situation from the professional point of view.

Our journey from King's Cross to Manchester was without exception the worst I have ever experienced at the hands of the Great Northern Railway. We were due at 4.30 and arrived at 7.50. How it was managed I could not make out. The luxury of the Midland Hotel would compensate, however, for a worse journey than that, and our troubles were soon forgotten in the discussion of a menu as elaborate and good as any you could find at the "Ritz," "Carlton," or "Savoy," to say nothing of the courteous welcome at the hands of my old friend Mr. Towle.

I was delighted to find myself in great form on Monday night after two rounds of golf in Trafford Park, and I believe I pleased the audience almost as much as I did myself. Through the kindness of Judge Parry I was a guest at the Brazenoze Club, a delightful rendezvous for a wet afternoon, with the certainty of a rubber almost any time after lunch. On my first visit I found a great gathering of the "law," but I was not only allowed to get away safely, but also to take a little plunder with me.

I had a bad attack of bridge fever one night, brought on by finding Arthur Collins was staying in the hotel, and he, Norman Salmond, de Frece, myself, and one other sat up until four o'clock at the game. We were all to have played golf the next day, but I was the only one to start, having promised to play my old friend George Lee, from whom I had a bad beating, which convinces me that one of two things must be done, either I must not indulge in late nights, or Lee's handicap must be lowered.

It was the turn of Norman Salmond and Constance Drever to develop bad throats in Liverpool, and we had two understudies to cope with. Winifred O'Connor surprised and gratified us all with the way in which she played the Princess at such very short notice, the trying song in the first act not presenting any difficulty to her, and the dialogue being well delivered.

It blew half a gale all the week, and golfing at Formby was almost more a toil than a pleasure, so that it was quite a relief to have to play a matinée one day.

It was one of the most womanly audiences I ever remember, and I have seen a good few; but after carefully searching all parts of the house I did at

last discover two men and one boy. This is a most
difficult kind of audience to give a really good performance to, for the reason that though highly appre-
ciative they cannot applaud or laugh sufficiently
loudly to make the players conscious of their
enjoyment.

In Nottingham I had what I believe is known as
a "succès fou" with a verse on a local topic, which I
had been recommended to allude to by a well-known
townsman. There had been a great agitation as to
the advisability of shutting up, or lighting up, the
Forest at sunset, neither of which propositions appeared
to suit the taste of the promenaders there, and it
seemed to relieve their minds greatly when I pointed
out in my verse that the quality of the gas supplied
was so inferior that should they decide to illuminate
the park in question it would make no material
difference.

Three of our "principal ladies" and de Frece and
myself went to supper at Mr. Payne's, the instigator
of the verse, and it was a great pleasure to meet unexpectedly one of the daughters of my old friend
Burnand, married to an excellent barrister and capital
fellow, Tinsley Linley. We had a very trying jaunt
on leaving the house about two o'clock. There was
only one cab available, so de Frece and I had to
escort the three ladies to their different addresses
before going to our hotel; this should have been
easy enough, but none of the three were quite
certain of the names of their streets, or their numbers

when we found the streets. The last one to be safely housed was Madge Vincent, and after driving round and round for an hour she exclaimed tearfully, "If he'd only go past the theatre I should know which way to go." At that moment the theatre hove in sight, and her house was visible from the cab window!

We had some great days at Hollinwell, a long course set in beautiful surroundings. I had a great match with Doctor Neilson which lives in my memory as being the best game I had played for a very long time, but their team was too strong for us.

We usually had a four-a-side match every week and generally did fairly well, but at Radyr, near Cardiff, a very beautiful course, we disgraced ourselves to the extent of losing every match; I myself only won one hole through my opponent driving into a very thick hedge.

The last week of the tour saw us at Portsmouth, a place of which I have always been fond, having pleasant recollections of many visits paid to my naval brother when he happened to be there. I made another experiment in the way of taking rooms here, with happier results than in former cases; but my catering seemed to leave something to be desired, as, having two or three people to lunch one day, and ordering " a decent slice of salmon," I found myself left with an enormous block of fish which was served at each and every meal untouched, until

I told the landlady that if I saw it again it would go out of the window.

The usual Monday exercise took place at Hayling, an interesting course though somewhat gravelly, and when approached via Eastney entailing a somewhat longer walk than I care to take before and after golfing.

There was a great naval show during the week in honour of Prince Fushimi, of which some three or four of us had an excellent view owing to the kindness of Flag Commander Macdonald, who took us on board the *Fire Queen*. The passing of the submarines was a most interesting feature, and I felt I would sooner be where I was than in the place of the sailor standing at attention right on the bows of these rapidly-moving sea-devils, with his feet apparently awash in the sea. Not the least pleasant incident was the arrival of two boatloads of cadets from Osborne, who swarmed on to the deck of the *Fire Queen* and were intensely interested spectators, and most chatty, pleasant boys.

Two or three of the most cheery and popular members of the Amāsis Syndicate came to Portsmouth to spend the last week of the tour with us, and by their genial hospitality enlivened the proceedings considerably. On the Friday night they entertained us with a supper and dance to follow at the Esplanade Hotel; possibly not the best night to have selected in view of a matinée and a "last performance" the next day, but who is going to refuse

M

an "evening's amusement" on account of the "morning's reflection"? Certainly none of the *Amāsis* company, and though some of us looked rather like wrecks in the morning, it was "all right at night." I think the audience were aware of its being a kind of fête performance, for though there were some marvellous vagaries indulged in, everything was taken in good part. I have before now met with the experience of an audience resenting that kind of fooling on the part of the players, and, to my mind, very justly, for after all they pay to see "the piece" unembroidered by personal jokes however humorous. Bouquets and presents of all kinds were flying from boxes to stage all the evening, and the climax came when I, as Pharaoh, having finished my song about "Lovely Woman," with its chorus of eight pretty girls, had to bring them all on again and pick up and hand them the eight bouquets lying on the stage, amongst which was a crown of laurel for myself—or perhaps it was "bays"; I am not sure. Even the High Priest, Norman Salmond, so far unbent from his normal dignity both "on" and "off" as to join in a plot to upset me. There was a quartette in which we all had to "toss up" for a fortune, and, according to the author, Ptolemy was the winner, but on this occasion they arranged it that the High Priest should win, which he did, supplemented with the remark, "That does your Majesty in the eye," thus causing an absolute *bouleversement* of the plot; but the piece was less upset than Norman himself, who was so overcome with excitement and delight at having "gagged" as to be incapable of completing the quartette. Mitton and de Frece added to the unexpected gaiety of the evening with a kind of miniature Hackenschmidt and Madrali effect, which left the former too breathless from laughter to sing, de Frece's wrestling being of the "little Marceline" type; and altogether, as I have tried to indicate, it was a merry, if disgraceful, presentation of Egyptian manners and behaviour.

Nor was the evening to conclude without the breaking of the law, for a small party of us assembled for a final supper at our host's hotel (of which I had better not give the name, or it may be raided); after which an hour or two of baccarat brought to a conclusion a most delightful tour, which will live in my memory as an extremely pleasant experience.

XV

Kennington and Coronet—Triple Bill

Towards the end of this very enjoyable tour certain inducements in the way of an interest in the profits "which might accrue" were made to me with regard to another excursion in the same part for the autumn, and having in view the business we had done in certain towns which we were to revisit, it presented itself as an opportunity not to be missed.

As the whole of the company had decided to follow the fortunes of *Amasis*, it appeared imperative to find some scheme of operations to keep things going during the hiatus of some eight or nine weeks—such a short period being difficult to fill up.

A plan of campaign was thought out and arranged by the stage manager, who, with consummate skill, persuaded us that a season of excerpts of well-known comic operas, combined with light one-act pieces, would prove highly popular at some two or three of the best-known suburban theatres.

What is perhaps more wonderful still is that he also impressed Mr. Robert Arthur with the same idea, and it was duly arranged that we should play a season of some six weeks at the Kennington and

Coronet theatres.   This was my first experience of
the commonwealth system, the said commonwealth
being composed of the business and stage managers,
Whitworth Mitton, Richard Green, and myself, the
other artists and all the choristers being engaged.   It
was an experiment that interested me immensely,
but at the same time one that I never wish to see
repeated with a like result.

The rehearsals for the initial week at Kennington
were held chiefly in large rooms attached to local
pubs, or odd corners at the theatre, but we eventually got well forward and started our venture with a
triple bill composed of a drama-ette called *The
King's Hat*, a one-act farce by B. C. Stephenson,
entitled *Faithful James*, and a compressed version of
La Mascotte, which was played in two scenes.   I had
not played Faithful James for some years, and was
pleased to renew his acquaintance, and I was also
cast for the King in *Mascotte*, so I had quite my
share of the work.   Madge Temple was excellent as
the Princess, but our Bettina was, unfortunately,
not equal to the task, and we had a great shuffling
of the pack the morning after our production.
Madge Temple, having played Bettina, had little
trouble in recalling it, and was admirable in the part,
while her rôle of the Princess was undertaken by
Winifred Macey with only one rehearsal and without
missing a word of the part or note of music, a really
wonderful achievement.   The Wednesday night performance was a vast improvement on the Monday,

but the mischief had been done, and the week ended badly from a financial point of view.

We opened on the following Monday at the Coronet with the same programme, with the intention of making a weekly change of at least two of the items. The scheme had been very largely announced and advertised, and yet a certain critic, in writing a notice of our second week, carefully ignored this and said, "Already the triple bill at the Coronet has been changed, and the dramatic ventures of Mr. Rutland Barrington do not seem to be any more successful now than when he opened and shut up the St. James's Theatre long ago." As he proceeded to "slate" one of the successful items of the programme, it is charitable to presume that he could not really have been present. In any case I feel sure that he is happily a unique specimen of that highly-intelligent and long-suffering body of men who are so ready to lend a helping hand to enterprise.

I had a rather quick change to make from the old waiter in *Faithful James* to the King in *Mascotte*, and one night, my usual valet being ill, I had a very nervous understudy who, for the final powdering of the King's face, handed me a puff full of neat boll Armenian, with the result that I was in a moment transformed into a Red Indian. It was an awful moment, as I had been called, and yet I had to wash it off, which I did incompletely and made a hasty appearance as a parti-coloured monarch. But this

was not so bad a change as I had the following week
when we put up the old farce called *Chiselling*, in
which I represented a statue and was smothered in
liquid white as to face, neck, and hands. It was an
awful mess, but as it is quite one of the best of the
old-fashioned kind of farces, it was worth the trouble,
and I got some extra fun out of it by threatening
my fellow-workers with embraces. Frank Lacy,
who was wearing his best Bond Street frock-coat,
would run anywhere to escape me, and poor Reggie
White, whose escape from my clutches the business
of the piece would not permit, was nightly reduced
almost to tears at the state of his black suit.

The second week of our season was rendered exceptionally interesting to me by reason of the production of a one-act musical drama of my own
writing, originally intended for Madame Esty at the
Coliseum. There were two songs for the soprano, a
duet and two or three choruses in it, all of which
were written by H. M. Higgs. The music obtained far better criticisms than the play, most
especially the duet, which was a fine piece of
writing, well delivered by Madge Temple and
Richard Green.

We (the composer and I) had an exasperating
experience, on the occasion of the first performance
of this ambitious trifle, at the hands of the orchestra.
After a very long and trying rehearsal we succeeded
in getting things fairly right, only to find at night
that certain members of the orchestra had sent depu-

ties; to my mind an unpardonable proceeding and one which nearly led to disaster.

I was naturally aware of the awful result before hearing the cause, and although I expressed my regret afterwards, I, at the moment, summed up the situation correctly when I told the conductor that I could have made better music with four cats and a tooth-comb. It improved as the week wore on, but the music was always handicapped, and I should like to hear it given a proper chance.

By this time the clouds on the commercial horizon of the enterprise were becoming more and more conspicuous. The first week at Kennington had resulted in a deficit, and the first week at Notting Hill in a larger one, and after holding a council of war it was decided to close down at the end of the third week. We were all, naturally, disappointed at the result of our hard labour, and the commonwealth was met in the kindest spirit by the artists and choristers, who were definitely engaged for a longer term, and had it in their power to make things very much worse had they desired to do so.

This ended my first experience of paying for the privilege of acting, writing, stage-managing, producing, and generally working very hard, and as, of course, my position entitled me to the largest percentage of the profits, it also carried with it the distinction of bearing the largest percentage of loss.

However, it was an experience I do not greatly regret, as it does no actor harm to vary the type of part he is in the habit of playing, in addition to which I had the pleasure of producing a piece of my own for which I charged no fee whatever; and last, but by no means least, the whole thing afforded for three weeks a living wage at least for many who would otherwise have been unemployed.

I am inclined to think that there was mismanagement somewhere, but it was certainly not on the part of Mr. Robert Arthur, who released us from the rest of our contract in a very handsome manner. I myself am disposed to think that "triple bills" are by no means so popular with the playgoing public as many people would have us believe, and my personal feeling is that I would always prefer to see and hear an entire opera or comedy than an abridged edition of one with a couple of one-act pieces as *hors-d'œuvre* and *relevé*.

That there was a time when this form of entertainment was to a certain extent popular is undoubtedly a fact, but with the advent of a more refined programme at music halls the new field has opened up a chance for both play and players which is eagerly seized upon, to the detriment, to a certain extent, of the theatre.

This is hardly a matter for regret, in view of the employment found for so many of the rank-and-file of the profession (as well as stars) who would otherwise find their long periods of "resting" a very undesirable occupation. I use the word "occupation" advisedly, as none but those who have undergone it know the amount of energy and restlessness demanded from the involuntary " rester."

I should like to see some of the enthusiasm devoted to the discussion of the need of a National Theatre applied to the establishment of a National Music Hall, where nothing but a good class of vaudeville and single turn should be introduced, and which, I believe, would be a sound commercial success if left in the hands of some two or three capable men as directors, with perhaps a small nucleus by way of a stock company, which could be relied upon in an emergency besides being the backbone of the entertainment. There is, of course, no need why this should be a "national" enterprise, the term being only suggested to me by the juxtaposition of ideas; in fact, I think on consideration it might turn out a severe handicap to what I believe would prove a great success.

XVI

AUGUST Bank Holiday found us once again on tour with *Amāsis*, commencing at Bristol, but our old golfing quartette was reduced by the loss of Norman Salmond and Mitton, who were not with us this time, and the piece also suffered by the loss of Reggie White as Ptolemy.

We managed, however, to put in an excellent morning on the links at Failand, where I had Chute as my partner against Glanfield and de Frece.

The surroundings at Failand are very beautiful, and once more awakened my desire to be able to sketch at the same time as I golfed, a feeling I have had on very many provincial courses.

I made a frantic endeavour to "count the house," being financially interested in the result, owing to my percentage, but although I tried it many times on this tour I never got very near the correct figures, my estimate usually being too high, possibly owing to the wish being father to the thought.

I found to my dismay that I had not entirely shaken off my throat affection, and towards the end of the week developed tonsilitis and more doctor's fees, which were not covered by my profit on the week.

187

We had a terribly early start on the Sunday, 7.30, being due in Dublin by dinner time, the only consolations being the beautiful scenery we travelled through in very leisurely fashion, and a magnificently breezy passage from Holyhead to Dublin, which did me a world of good, but left me very tired.

Almost the first greeting I received in Dublin was a wish from the mouth of the porter who assisted my servant to put the luggage on a cab, to the effect that he hoped that Dublin "would not see us again for a long time"! This struck me as so unlike the proverbial Irish hospitality that I inquired of my servant the amount of his fee, which he told me had been the usual shilling, sternly rejected by the porter, who, however, eventually ran after the cab and accepted it ; he was evidently an Irish Pooh Bah, and thought his "insult" a "light one."

The Exhibition was being held during the week, and the most popular feature was the band of the Coldstream Guards, a fact which appeared to puzzle my companion, de Frece, considerably, until I pointed out that they are a band of Englishmen originally raised in a village on the border of Scotland, which none of them have ever seen ; and if that is not Irish, what is ?

I was on the sick-list in Dublin from the time of arrival until the Thursday night, a period that might well have been extended but for the skill of Dr. Lennon and the excellent nursing of Mrs. Roland Cunningham ; and Thursday was memorable on account of the first solid food for a week, and that was an Irish solid, so to speak, consisting of one egg, on which I played that night (of course, I played on the stage, not on the egg), but I managed to get through.

There was a great influx of stout clerics in the hotel during two days of the week, and the one or two ascetic-looking, thin Churchmen among them impressed me for some reason with the feeling that, in the event of a "consultation," I should select the attenuate in preference to the rotund. I wonder if they experience more trouble with the obese heathen, and if so, why? I intended to have asked one of them to enlighten me on the point, but on the morning I wished to do so they had all disappeared.

We were all much interested in reading about the great strike in Belfast, then in full swing, where we were due on the following Monday, and it was with no little pleasure that towards the end of the week we read that it was over, and we therefore started on the Sunday with light hearts.

Our lightsomeness suffered a certain depression on the journey, however, as the railway company sneered at our desire for a special train, and the one we travelled in was specially awful. I also noticed that here, as in England, passengers are almost invariably regarded as undesired interlopers, to be dealt with severely and harried and hustled at the sweet will of the railway underlings.

We had two very good days' golf at Portmarnock,

and the passage across the arm of the sea in cabs was quite an exciting experience; one does not often have the chance of driving in a cab with one's feet in the sea!

I had one slice of luck in Dublin, the week's business bringing me a nice little sum on my percentage arrangement, my joy at the news being mitigated to some extent by the fact that the surplus all went to balance the nights on which I was unable to play.

Belfast was quite quiet we found, but the whole town was patrolled by stern-faced warriors of the Sussex Regiment, some of them very youthful-looking, but no worse soldiers for that, and they had been through some rougher times than had been made public, as I gathered from a chat I had with two or three of them; it must be a difficult thing to refrain from retaliation when bombarded with stones and huge slabs of pavement, as they were.

Roland Cunningham and I had a delightful day at Newcastle, Co. Down, only marred by the fact of the strike having changed its locale and attacked the waiters at the Slieve Donard Hotel, making the getting of lunch a matter of some uncertainty; but what mattered lunch with such fine golf at hand, and the best day in point of weather since we left town!

A perfectly charming little incident occurred as we were leaving the club-house. I saw at some little distance, coming over the sandhills, a little boy and girl dressed in Red Indian costume, all complete up to the train of feathers on the head and down to the moccasins, and both carried bows and arrows.

When they were within some sixty yards I pretended great fear, and crouched down; Roland took up his cue promptly and did the same; and to our delight the little Indians "stalked" us! After runing a little distance I fell exhausted and the little girl walked round me, arrow fitted to bow, with intent to shoot me dead; the arrow was fortunately blunt, as she eventually shot me well below the belt, when I shuddered and died, whereupon she ran away shrieking with delight. Roland had meanwhile escaped with his scalp and we waved a farewell to our foes and parted without a word spoken on either side.

We experienced a very striking contrast to the hospitality of our reception at Dublin station when we went on the Saturday of this week to Carnalea to play a golf match of five aside between Amāsis and the Carnalea Club as represented by Messrs. Agnew, Black, Phillips, Rogers, and Kamche. It was a close contest, four of the matches being halved, while we lost the odd one.

The festivities which followed this exciting result were of a somewhat potent nature, and so prolonged as to threaten some danger to the evening's performance of the opera. Stanhope (our manager) and I held a council of war and decided to invite all our opponents to occupy a box that night; and the proposition being received with acclamation, there only remained just enough time for a stirrup-cup and a rush for the train, so that all danger was averted.

We took ship that night, after work, for Heysham, and it was most interesting to watch the gradual filling up of the steamer with ourselves, certain other passengers, many cows, and last but not least the gallant Sussex Regiment returning home with the same high courage with which it had left, strongly manifested by performances on mouth-organs, concertinas, and the human voice.

The "last load" was our *Amāsis* scenery, and when later on I went for a stroll round the deck I found portions of my royal palace, temple, and sphinxes occupied by the slumbering warriors, one of whom was extremely snug in the depths of Pharaoh's royal chair; the majority of them slept hand in hand with some favoured comrade, and in more than one instance the boots of one man reposed on the face of another without causing any apparent inconvenience,

The Leeds audiences, where we played next, have established a reputation for being somewhat difficult to please, in spite of, or perhaps because of, being possessed of a keen sense of humour; in fact, I have heard one of the theatres in the town described as "The Comedian's Grave"; but it is only fair to state that they showed no lack of appreciation during our visit.

One of our principal artists, who was under notice to leave on the Saturday, elected to vanish mysteriously two days in advance, a somewhat unwarrantable proceeding, and one which might have seriously inconvenienced us had not the understudy been ready and efficient.

We again finished the week with a golf match against six of the Headingely Club, in which we were badly defeated, the only winner on our side being an importation in the shape of Frank Curzon, who was staying at Harrogate, where he had evolved quite a strong game by avoiding the waters.

The following week, while at Bradford, we played over what in my humble opinion is the best inland course I have ever seen, Hawksworth to wit, the greens being nothing short of perfection. We had a very narrow margin to catch our return train; and the cab not arriving, we were reduced to stealing a private motor-car, instigated thereto by the captain of the club, Dr. Honeybone, who seemed sure the owner would not mind. I hope he did not, and am glad of the chance of thanking him.

I was agreeably surprised to find an invitation from the Mayor to lunch with him at the town hall on the Wednesday. It appears that it was a weekly function established by him, the courtesy of an invitation to which he extends to any well-known visitor whom he may wish to meet; a very happy thought, which I found, on signing the visitors' book, had been appreciated by several of my fellow actors, including Sir Henry Irving.

The Mayor (Mr. J. L. Godwin) was in hourly ex-

N

pectation of being created Lord Mayor of Bradford, and I promised that if the news arrived during our visit, and he would be present at the theatre the night it arrived, I would evolve and sing a special verse to fit the occasion.

I thought no more of this, and on the Friday, after a long day's golf, I was informed on arriving at the theatre that the news had arrived and the Lord Mayor was in the box! I managed, however, to carry out my part of the bargain, wrote the verse during the interval, and sang it with great success. I found, on reaching the hotel, that a note from him had miscarried, and I ought to have had due notice.

A little brass tablet on one of the dressing-room doors brought me some sad thoughts when I saw that it recorded the fact of its being the room that Sir Henry Irving used during his last appearances on the stage, and a picture rose in my mind of the last impressive scene of all in Westminster Abbey, and the (to me) appalling character of part of the music.

From Bradford to Southport was a pleasant move, and the weather being glorious, we had a great week's pleasure, if somewhat unsatisfactory from a business point of view.

Mixed bathing was indulged in by most of our company, though it is difficult to really " bathe " when the depth of water for a mile or so out does not exceed two feet. We played sea-football one afternoon, and most uproarious fun it was, ending in a " scrum " in which every player flopped down in the water; one imaginative person declared that when I fell there was a tidal wave, in spite of which a part of me still emerged like an island, but I fancy the statement was prompted by jealousy of my figure.

John Doran, our tenor, had only been able to secure an extremely large costume intended for a lady, and as he went down the hundred yards of sand between him and the sea, the wind inflated his dress in a most ludicrous manner, causing de Frece to ask politely, " What time do you go up ? "

It was perhaps as well that we fixed on the luncheon hour for the match, when very few strangers were about, though the manager regretted that he had not had time to get out some handbills advertising the attraction !

As a proof of the (occasional) efficacy of "gagging," I may instance a night at Southport when, owing to some misunderstanding, the eight girls wanted for my song, " Lovely Woman," were on the stage in other costumes, when they should have been changing. I noticed it, sent them off, and then de Frece and myself lengthened out the scene until they were ready. The introduced lines went very well, but best with the company on the stage, who were, of course, in the secret and glad to welcome a deviation from the routine.

From Southport to Edinburgh was rather a far cry, taking us from 10.30 till 5 to accomplish, but, owing to the forethought of Mrs. Roland Cunningham, an experienced traveller, was rendered thoroughly comfortable by means of a lunch and tea worthy of the best hotel cuisine; in addition to which there was awaiting us a delightful dinner party at the house of my old friend and golf opponent Mr. Law, of *The Scotsman*, to which Mr. and Mrs. Cunningham, Mr. and Mrs. Stanhope, Madge Vincent, Winifred O'Connor, Winnie Macey, de Frece, and myself were bidden.

The little concert which followed was a pleasant holiday for us, though we were the makers of the melody, assisted by our host himself.

On the Monday I drove up to the Braids with Cunningham, just to prospect, rehearsal having occupied most of the day. What a course to be able to play over for twopence! It seems a pity we have nothing like it near London.

While walking from the hotel to my work that night a very pretty little girl passed me, and in doing so dropped a glove. I picked it up and handed it to her, when she promptly dropped the other one. I handed her that also, and being under the impression that it might be a new game, or some Scotch custom, I said quite simply, "What will you drop next?" Upon which she ran away like a rabbit. Being uncertain whether I ought to run also, I gave myself the benefit of the doubt and walked away in the opposite direction.

Edinburgh, as all know, is a grand centre for golf, and I was anxious to show one or two of my companions the beauties of the links at Archerfield, where at the time Mr. Herbert Gladstone and the Hon. Alfred Lyttelton were enjoying a holiday. Being an old opponent of the former, a note asking for permission to play brought me not only acquiescence but in addition an invitation to lunch for myself and my three friends; and a great day we had, though it took me eight strokes to do a certain hole which I had once captured in one.

A prolonged lunch left no time for another round of golf, so the interval between that and train-catching was occupied with the usual concert, varied on this occasion with some glees from Gilbert-and-Sullivan operas, in which Mrs. Gladstone was our leading soprano.

This pleasant golf picnic was followed by a serious day at New Luffness (as far as golf went, of course), which nearly ended in our being minus a tenor for that night. I got back in my host's (George Law's) car in good time, but the second car had a bad puncture soon after starting, on a lonely road, which was mended by stuffing the tyre with grass, necessitating a stop at every "house of call" on the road to "see if it was standing the strain." It appeared to have done so, very much to the added merriment of its load of passengers, my friend Doran, the tenor in question, being quite light-hearted over his love troubles in *Amāsis*.

In one particular scene in the second act I was in the habit of using for a gag that which I fondly hoped was a fairly good Scotch accent; anyhow it invariably produced a good laugh, but some evil genius in the shape of a good friend recommended me to preface the gag with " Hoots ! " by way of strengthening the imitation. I tried it once, lost my breath entirely with the effort to say "Hoots!" and with it the accustomed laugh.

We fixed up an early journey to Glasgow, intending to take a train out into the suburbs after lunch, but after getting every one out of bed at an unprecedented hour we found, on arriving at Glasgow, that there were no trains going anywhere, so Edinburgh would have been preferable.

There is a peculiarity about the hotel I always go to in Glasgow which I have never noticed elsewhere, which is, that an abnormal number of wedding parties assemble there for breakfasts, dinners, balls, and occasionally for the ceremony itself.

There are more often than not two such affairs daily, and I have several times seen three in full swing, all of which gives a startling variety of dishes, dangerous to dyspeptics, in a profusion which is only excelled by the confetti which covers the whole of the entrance floor and stairs, and is never entirely got rid of.

One particular party attracted my attention strongly on account of the terrible air of dejection displayed by all except a small boy and girl, who were flirting outrageously in happy disregard of the gloom surrounding their seniors.

The Glaswegian youth is evidently inclined to be

precocious, at least I gather so from the story told me by two of our youngest and prettiest ladies of the chorus, who on their way home after work one night were followed by two youths who were persistent in their efforts to start a conversation. On being firmly told that their society was so little desired that they were an absolute nuisance, one of them remarked, " Well, if you won't talk to us you will lose our patronage ! "

We had a very delightful supper party one night at the Palette Club, our hosts being David Kemp and Doctor Maclure, followed by a capital impromptu "smoker" for which I acted as chairman, prompted as to the "local talent" by Maclure, who unearthed for our pleasure a really delightful artist of the name of Rankin.

There was a somewhat extraordinary mixture travelling by our train (and others) on the Sunday, consisting of two "musical" companies, one drama, a sketch, some dozen music-hall artists, and eight or nine Chinese stokers going somewhere to stoke, I presume.

On our return visit to Hull we had a great golf match at Brough against four of Yorkshire's well-known lady players, and as they honoured us by occupying a box at the theatre the same night we were, of course, compelled to introduce some "golf-gags," which must have sounded odd coming from Egyptians ; however, they amused those in the secret, and no harm was done to the play.

This town furnished me with a proof of my argument, that in bringing a piece round a second time it is dangerous to make many alterations in the company, unless, of course, you bring stars in the place of ordinary artists. There were other things as well to account for the reduction in our receipts, notably the death of Lord Nunburnholme and the municipal elections, but, all the same, I think his townspeople missed Norman Salmond, and I am sure we did.

I mean no reflection on the performance of the part by Mr. Fox, an old Carl Rosa artist and good actor, but it is an undoubted fact that most people consider the first exponent of any part to be the best, however well it may be played by the successor.

Being in Liverpool shortly after this, during a race week, I was anxious to see the course for the first time, but the weather was against it until the Saturday, when we had, of course, a matinée; however, I just managed to see two races, got back to my hotel to lunch, and arrived at the theatre at two o'clock, not bad going. I backed the winner of the first race, and venture to hope that I shall some day back the same horse to win the Grand National, it being that smart young chaser, Cackler.

They have an odd custom at this hotel of putting one's letters on the top of the boots that have been left out overnight for cleaning, which is all very well if you have only one pair of boots, but the custom played me a bad trick, as thus: I was expecting important letters from town on Friday morning (it would be on a Friday such a thing would happen), and up to Sunday morning there was no sign of them. I pointed out to my servant which boots I would wear, and when he picked them up out fell the expected letters! One of them contained a request that I would go to town that day, and fortunately I had just time to alter my arrangements and travel to London instead of Middlesbrough, but it was a near thing, and I look into my boots now every morning when away from home.

We had a great day on the sands at Redcar, about twenty of the company joining in a picnic, and the only conveyance to hold us all from the station to the hotel was a lorry, which we sat round with dangling feet, much to the amazement of the natives and the joy of the dogs of the place, which pursued us all the time and saw us off at the end of the day. I ventured to join in a game of rounders, having memories of my old sprinting days conjured up, and felt rather proud of scoring two rounders, but my pride was dashed when some one remarked that when running I looked rather like the hind part of an elephant. How are the mighty fallen!

From Middlesbrough to Nottingham was a somewhat circuitous route, and de Frece and Stanhope thought they would prefer to do it in a motor-car. They started some three hours before us, and were on the platform at York at one o'clock to welcome us as the train steamed in. When leaving again we agreed to wait dinner for them at Nottingham, and we accordingly did so, but we did not wait until they arrived, which was at 5.30 on the Monday afternoon! We had a better night than they.

This journey was eclipsed by our very next one, right up to Sunderland, and they appeared to be mending the line everywhere, which made us only two and a half hours late. This did not matter so much to us in the train, but it was hard on the station-master at Durham, where I had arranged to stop the special to pick up my sister; it appeared that the station had to be opened exclusively for her benefit by the station-master himself, who attended in tall hat, frock-coat, and white gloves as befitting the ceremony. At the end of the long wait (over two hours) the "suite" of nephews and one niece were exhausted, but my sister and the station-master preserved their gallant bearing and betrayed no impatience.

The Bolton Wanderers were playing Sunderland on the Saturday, and as they stayed in the hotel at Roker, where some of our party were, I had an opportunity of making their acquaintance. I found them a pleasant, unassuming lot of men, very musical (we had a two hours' sing-song before the match), and capital footer players, as I discovered at the match in the afternoon, their "outside right" being fast enough to have given him a show even in the Stadium.

The mention of the Stadium reminds me that I saw the great "disqualification" race for the four hundred yards, and I shall never forget the shout which rose from the spectators at the celebrated bend, and came along with the runners right up to where the winning tape had been broken by the judges on the signal from the umpire down the course. It was a thousand pities that the whole race was not run in strings, though perhaps to have ordered such a proceeding might have argued a suspicion, that could not possibly have been harboured, that something untoward was likely to happen. Whether accident or design I should not like to say; but the fortunate presence of the ubiquitous photographer clearly proved to all that the tracks of one runner went right across those of the man just behind him. I have never seen such excitement over a foot race before, and never wish to see it again, if attributable to the same cause.

After playing *Amāsis* for a week in Oldham, the first time I ever had the pleasure of being in the town, we forgathered for our final Sunday journey to town by the Great Central. Living in Manchester, and only going over to Oldham in time for work, I naturally saw very little of the place, and my one recollection is of an enormous arc-lamp fixed in the centre of the dress-circle so as to throw its light on to the stage; it was at first intensely disconcerting, being of so powerful a nature that it seemed to hit one with light, and absolutely prevented one's seeing anything of the house while on the stage.

Mingled feelings of joy at returning to London,

and regret at finishing a pleasant tour, occupied my mind during our last journey, untainted by any presentiment of such a disaster as nearly befell us just outside town. We were running at about fifteen miles an hour, I should imagine, when we felt a series of severe jerks, followed by one worse than the rest, and then a sudden stoppage; it was evident something had happened, and all heads were out of windows at once. There was a certain amount of tension observable in most of us, and one or two girls threatened to become hysterical, but at the sight of a gang of platelayers standing on the line, who replied to a general question "if there had been an accident?"—yes!—the atmosphere was cleared by a roar of laughter on Winifred O'Connor (Princess Amāsis) inquiring, "Can I be of any help?"

Roland Cunningham and I, with a feeling on us of grave responsibility, got out on the line to make inquiries, the result of which was to establish the fact that some forty feet or more of the rails were "up," and the men were carrying across the last rail to be put down when to their horror our train came round the bend.

Their schedule showed no train due at all for some hours (ours had been forgotten in some mysterious way), and though they had sent a man down the line as look-out, he had only a flag, which was not of much use in the dark.

But for the courage, resource, and watchfulness of our driver, Ogden, of Gorton, Manchester, who saw the flag and immediately reversed his engine, it is terrible to think what might have happened to us all; as it was the engine had run through the sleepers like matchwood, was on its side, and the baggage wagon immediately behind the tender had mounted right on top of it.

When I remember that as a rule the saloon which held all the principal artists came next to the engine, it seems providential that on this one occasion an exception was made.

I had quite a long chat with Driver Ogden, who naturally seemed much upset about it, but it was evidently no fault of his, and when assured that no one was more than badly shaken up his equanimity was restored.

Many of us climbed up the bank and made the best of our way to our destinations, the remainder waiting till another train came alongside and transported them bag and baggage to Marylebone; but it was a great disappointment to the crowd of friends and relations assembled to greet our return, to say nothing of the brass band engaged.

There is always a feeling of regret on parting with a piece in which one has played a "grateful" part for so long a time as I had that of Pharaoh, and it was deepened on this occasion by the idea that was in my mind that in the hands of any well-known and capable London manager *Amāsis* would still be running in town.

Theatrical business is a great lottery, and how

often we hear of the winning ticket having been sold or even given away, in the shape of constant refusals to see "any good" in plays submitted, which afterwards found the fortune of some plucky if haphazard producer.

I myself have at the present time certain plays, the titles and subjects of which wild horses shall not persuade me to divulge, which have been "submitted" in various quarters, received (in some cases) hearty encomiums, but yet seem fated not to see production until the aforesaid haphazard explorer comes along. I can only hope for his sake that he will hasten his appearance, as it is my firm intention to burn a considerable amount of type-covered sheets next week, and though the cheap cynic would naturally say that is all they are fit for, I know of one person at least who holds a contrary opinion.

XVII

TOWARDS the end of this tour I received a letter
from Leedham Bantock suggesting that he should
book me for a trial trip with a sketch, which he also
recommended should be founded on a one-act play
of mine called *Mummydom*, which was produced at
Penley's Theatre some years ago. It had a cast of
six characters, and besides solos for the soprano,
tenor, and comedian, there were two or three concerted
numbers in music, all of which had been written by
Wilfrid Bendall.

The piece met with a certain success when
produced, so I was inclined to think something
might be done with it. I compressed it into about
half an hour's work and cut out the tenor part
entirely, on the advice of Roland Cunningham,
which was really disinterested of him as I wanted
him to play it. I only had a fortnight in town to
get things in train, and as Christmas week was part
of it there was not much time to do it in. Also it is
a bad time of year to get a stage to rehearse on, and
but for the kindness of Mr. Glenister in lending me
the Pavilion I could not have done it. Then we had

to unearth the scenery and costumes which had been stowed away for years at Hudson's Depository, and were only found three days before I was due to leave London for Liverpool. However, it was all complete at last, and Sunday, 29 December, 1907, saw me leave for the provinces for the first time with my own company—four artists besides myself, a stage manager, five ladies as choristers, and my valet, who was to play a policeman. We had, originally, six choristers, but as it made our number up to thirteen I was superstitious enough to reduce them to five, and even then we started thirteen, as the scoring was unfinished and the composer came to Liverpool to complete it. I thoroughly enjoyed the journey, having always been rather fond of travelling about, and we arrived in Liverpool in great spirits, looking forward to Monday night. I dined on the Sunday at the Racquet Club with A. G. Tait, a brother of the famous champion golfer and no mean exponent himself, who always provides me some pleasant days at Formby; and made an early retirement to rest full of happiness, hope, and hospitality.

The next morning I paid an early visit to the Empire to see how things shaped, and received a shock—the first of a series and rather a severe one. I, of course, knew that my scenery was in no way elaborate; indeed, it only consisted of two cloths. but I thought it would be sufficient when "masked in" by the proscenium wings; but to say I was horrified is not putting it too strongly when I saw two miserable little rags hanging in the centre of the somewhat large stage and was met by the stage manager's inquiry, " Is this all you have, Mr. Barrington ? " To my feeling of horror succeeded an access of shame at making such a poverty-stricken appearance, and then came the awful thought—What was to be done ? I would most willingly have disappeared down a trap if there had been one, but there was not, and the situation had to be met. The whole of the staff were most kind and helpful, and it was fixed up at last; but fancy my feelings at being obliged to mask in the catacombs with wings of autumn woods in England; and I was lucky to get them, too, for they only provide a limited amount of scenery in most halls, and that mostly interiors.

The following day we scoured Liverpool and eventually found some rock-wings at the Theatre Royal, which were most kindly lent to me, and I also ordered an entirely new scene, which was promised me for the following Monday at Birmingham, and came as promised. I began to learn things on the first Monday at Liverpool, and I never left off while on the halls. The first thing I learnt was the delightful courtesy shown, combined with a readiness to do anything to promote one's comfort on the part of every one, from the manager to the call-boy; not only in Liverpool, be it understood, but in every hall it has been my privilege to visit. The conductors of the different orchestras have a very difficult task, but I never found one who was not anxious to do all in his power to help, and I

o

have had numbers composed, scored, copied, and rehearsed all in two or three days. Among other things which did not take me very long to learn was the important position occupied by the artist who is "top of the bill." On the Monday night I was disappointed to find that my sketch was the absolutely last turn, but I was told by several of the other artists that "it's the custom here," so felt more at ease. However, I was so much worried by the people leaving before the sketch was over, not because they did not like it but because it was close on "closing time" for the public-houses, that on the second night I got it transferred some three places earlier, much to the advantage of my sketch and, as I found after, the annoyance of one of the other items, whose very indignant remonstrances at being "pushed about" were met by the unanswerable argument—"Mr. Barrington is the top of the bill and must be considered."

I felt considerably flattered to see many of the other artists standing in the wings frequently to watch my sketch, but the feeling was, to a certain extent, discounted on discovering that the attraction was the song so admirably given by Winifred O'Connor.

The dressing-room accommodation was rather a shock to me after the luxury I had been in the habit of thinking indispensable at Daly's and other theatres; but worse than that were the draughty corridors. We all caught colds, and mine, of course, developed into my old enemy laryngitis, and by the Saturday night I was nearly speechless.

On Sunday it took us five solid hours to get to Birmingham, snow and sleet pursuing us all the way; and I went straight to the hospital for a specialist, that is to say, on the telephone, for nothing would have tempted me to leave the generous warmth of the hotel fireside. After I had been subjected to the usual " treatment " at his hands, I went to bed firmly convinced that unless the frost gave I should not sing on the Monday night. How thankful I was on waking to find the rain coming down in sheets and no sign of snow is perhaps easier to tell than understand.

What small accumulation of success we had acquired in Liverpool evaporated under the trying conditions which obtained in Birmingham, for I was ill the whole week, twice going direct from bed to work ; indeed, but for the consideration shown me by Mr. Foster, the local manager, with regard to my personal comfort, I doubt if I could have pulled through.

My personal friend and agent, Leedham Bantock, came down to see the sketch and make suggestions, and our council included Foster, who had some useful hints to impart, the result being that we decided on such radical alterations in the way of plot, dresses, dialogue, and numbers as took a fortnight to arrange and rehearse, thus most fortunately escaping Edinburgh (where the sketch went extremely

well in its original form) ; and being tried for the
first time on the Monday at Glasgow, where the
changes elaborated at such expense of time, trouble,
and money so nearly killed the sketch that for the
" second house " the same night I reverted to the
original form, with the exception of retaining a
bright little number I had added, rather on the lines
of the *Six Little Wives,* and possibly on that account
quite a success.

It was a tremendous effort to get all our scenery
and dresses out of the theatre and down to the
station in time to catch the eleven o'clock train on
Saturday night to Edinburgh, the alternative being
one which would have necessitated our travelling
from about five o'clock on Sunday evening till about
ten the next morning. These journeys form some of
the difficulties and inconveniences that music-hall
artists are subjected to, owing, of course, to there
not being enough passengers to warrant a special,
and the commissariat department is entirely a personal affair, it being the exception to find any food
en route. I learned another lesson during this week
in Edinburgh, which I found extremely useful. There
was a very important sort of dream-medley sketch,
which appeared to necessitate the services of quite a
number of artists, being played, and having been
told by several people that they could not make out
what it was about, and this view being evidently
shared by the audience, in spite of which there were
three or four " recalls " every night, I felt impelled

to seek the solution of such apparent contradiction. With this object in view I saw the sketch twice my self and came to the conclusion that it really was difficult of comprehension, but as to the " recalls," the chief artist concerned supplied the lesson I refer to, for I noticed that however much or little the applause at its conclusion, the curtain was invariably raised and lowered some three or four times, and eventually a kind of spurious enthusiasm was actually evoked. I applied this lesson at once to my own sketch, restricting the " curtain-work " to twice, however, and was delighted to find it eminently successful, and also most encouraging to the members of my little company; surely a proof that it is quite the right thing to do.

What a nightmare the first performance in Glasgow was, though! The alterations, from which we all expected so much, necessitated a rapid change of dress in the wings between Reggie White and myself, and the two ladies left on the stage were instructed to " gag " if there should be a wait. There was an awful wait, but no " gags " were forthcoming, and the piece ended so tamely that even the double " recall " was no tonic to our depression. Fortunately, there was just time between the two houses to revert to the old order of things, the wisdom of which was fully justified by the result. In the discarded version I made one entrance in a dress strongly resembling a certain well-known poster; at least we all thought so, but apparently the audience did not notice it, as I failed to raise a laugh when I quoted the words on the poster, " Ma mither winna gie me ony mair Oxo !" Possibly my Scotch was faulty, though I hardly think that was entirely to account for it, as on the Saturday night, being the Burns Birthday Celebration, I wrote and sang a special verse, with a few Scotch words in it, which went like " hot cakes."

From Glasgow to the Coliseum, London, was another far cry, made in a most leisurely manner on account of the numerous portions of the train which dropped off at one station to be replaced by others which had to be carried some distance and then thrown off to look after themselves, the most prolific meeting-place being Crewe, where we spent some two hours and more shunting on to different sets of metals until they eventually found one that led to London, much to the relief of the officials (not to mention ourselves !), who appeared to have suddenly tired of playing trains with us.

By the time we had reached our Coliseum week the sketch had really got into first-class working order, and I venture to say that nothing in the programme was more heartily received ; but our hopes of a continuance for a few weeks were dispelled by the fact that, owing to the initial performances not having aroused sufficient enthusiasm, certain dates kept for us had been filled up and we were doomed to be homeless wanderers. In this way I learned yet another lesson, for had I had the foresight to have invited other managers to see the sketch it might have appealed to them as "the very thing they wanted." Lessons are usually costly affairs, and this was no exception to the rule.

Having arranged to return to the Savoy in April, there was no occasion to look for permanent work in the meanwhile; but to keep my hand in I determined to give a week's trial to a sketch written by Leedham Bantock, entitled *Man the Lifeboat*, the character of the old sailor who had been "coxswain of the boat for forty-three years" appealing to me very strongly, with its mixture of comedy and homely pathos. We both felt certain that it would prove very acceptable to the public, who seem to have a special fondness for the sea and sailors, and especially love a storm and a rescue.

Julian Hicks painted me a delightful cottage interior, with a large diamond-paned window showing the distant lighthouse and the storm clouds and an angry sea, contrasting well with the cosy firelight inside the room, where the three old cronies sat wassailing. I am not quite clear as to how the ancients of old "wassailed," but we did it for a whole week on good English beer, and the after-effects were not so serious as those one reads about.

I searched London in vain to find a dozen cork jackets, sou'-westers, and oilskins as worn by life-boatmen, for they naturally had to be the genuine article. However, I called in the assistance of my friend Flag-Commander W. B. Macdonald, who kindly scoured Portsmouth until he found me exactly what I wanted; and a most picturesque effect was obtained at the end of the sketch with all the men in their rough-weather kit, including the coxswain's daughter, who had taken her father's place and steered the boat.

With the addition of a little more comedy, it is my intention to make a prolonged tour with this sketch one of these days, the Fates being propitious, and it is just the kind of character I should like to make an appearance with in America.

My two " old cronies " were played by Danby and Bennett, the latter of whom was essaying a part for the first time, though having for some years been a chorister, and they were both excellent in two totally different types of hardy mariner. Frank Lacy was the young hero who was wrecked and saved by his sweetheart, and Terriss himself could not have been more breezy, but he was greatly chagrined that he had no part in the " wassailing," and as the arrangement of the " properties " came into his department as stage manager, the enormous jug of beer, off which the froth had to be blown by one of the men, was found to be fitted with the necessary false bottom somewhat nearer the neck than it might have been under other circumstances.

With this sketch I found, to my great gratification, that the lesson I had learned as to " recalls " was quite superfluous, as they were a natural sequence of the happy conclusion. The lifeboat is now in dry-dock, being overhauled and put in readiness for next autumn, when the stormy winds do blow.

XVIII

I FELT very much honoured at being asked to propose the toast of the " Savoy Lovers " at the celebration dinner given by the O.P. Club, with Gilbert
as the guest of the evening. The "Savoy Lovers"
naturally included all who have been there and enjoyed such delightful evenings, but they were
particularized on this memorable evening in the
persons of our hosts, that is to say, the members of
the Old Playgoers' Club ; therefore, to my mind,
adding to the compliment. I acquitted myself with
my usual after-dinner brilliancy, the only part of
the speech I had absolutely prepared being the
peroration, which took the form of a few lines ending
in praise of the genial Carl Hentschel, an old friend
of mine and a prime mover in establishing the club
which was entertaining us. On this occasion his
presence was " essential," that was how I rhymed
him, but later on, when he was in such trouble over
the robbery of the royal miniatures, and I had a
verse about him (at the Coliseum), he rhymed with
" providential," both of which propositions seem to
indicate the character of the man.

I sat next but one to Gilbert at the dinner, and

although he seemed much as usual, I thought I detected a slight feeling of nervousness at the ordeal of speech-making which lay before him. On the other hand what I took for nervousness may have been the shadow of the added dignity which he was so soon to assume with the honour of knighthood, for there was certainly no nervousness displayed in the delivery of his speech, to which we all listened with intense interest.

The inevitable note of sadness was struck in the absence of Arthur Sullivan. Fancy the enthusiasm which would have been aroused had we had the good fortune to toast the composer as well as the author, but failing this we had the consolation of his music, which is with us for all time and the freshness of which is perennial.

The mention of his name at this dinner brought most vividly to my mind that last impressive scene in the Chapel Royal when I attended his obsequies, and the whole of the music, exquisitely written, and exquisitely sung by the choir of which as a boy he had been a member, was due, every bar of it, to the fertile brain hidden in that wooden casket, never to hear it more, that at least being the accepted idea, but difficult of belief. The feeling this idea gave me was inexpressibly sad.

Mr. Sidney Dark, the president of the club, in the course of his excellent speech, told us that it had been suggested to him that the mention of Sullivan's name might strike a sad note that would be undesirable at such a festival, but, as he so well put it, "it would not be possible to toast Savoy Opera and avoid mention of one of the hands that made it, and if he is aware, as I think he may be, of this gathering, he cannot fail to be glad that not only is his memory kept green in our hearts, but that his work with its lilting memories is designed to delight generations yet unborn."

Gilbert paid some very high compliments in his turn both to the past and present Savoyards, of whom there were a goodly number present, including George Grossmith, Richard Temple, and Jessie Bond of the original band, with whom it seemed strange to me to forgather after so many years had elapsed. I had at this time no idea that I should ever again enlist under the old banner, and naturally less that on doing so I should find myself the sole representative of the old originals"; but not having met Jessie for so long I found myself looking at her somewhat critically with a view to the possibility of a reunion, and I determined in my mind that she looked unlikely to forsake the evident prosperity of her present existence for the hard-working sphere in which she had formerly shone.

I had no more than two or three words with her on this occasion, but we were to meet unexpectedly in the autumn of 1907 and pass a pleasant day or two. I was playing in Nottingham in *Amāsis*, and one morning during the week was debating between golf and going to a meet of Earl Harrington's hounds, some seven miles out of the town. I have always been fond of attending meets and seeing hounds, if possible, find and go away, and this was a chance not to be missed. I was asking the hall-porter about trains when I was overheard by Colonel Birkin, who was just going out; on realizing my proposed programme he very kindly lent me his motor for the day, and I started off on my jaunt. On arriving at Thurgaton Priory I left the car in the drive and walked up to the house just as the hunt assembled in front of it to be photographed, when, to my surprise, I heard a voice exclaiming with evident pleasure and surprise, " Why, it's Barry !" The owner of the voice was Jessie Bond, and we spent the best part of the day careering round the lanes after the field, and owing to the intimate know-ledge of the country possessed by Colonel Birkin's chauffeur, we saw a good deal of sport.

This was not the only turn he did us both, as on Saturday, when Jessie came to lunch with me in order to go to our matinée, we had decided to back a certain horse for the Liverpool Autumn Cup, and he advised us to change the name on the telegram for one which proved the ultimate winner.

I have strayed somewhat far from the Savoy and dinner in company with Jessie (excuse enough surely), and now wish to return to it to mention a graceful little act on the part of Henry Lytton which pleased me very much. There was a short selection of songs and quartettes given after dinner, between the toasts (Norfolk Megone's excellent orchestra having given us a treat all through the long menu), and I saw that Lytton was announced to sing the Vicar's song from *The Sorcerer.* I rather felt that I ought to sing it myself, but I was not on the programme, for the reason that I had a speech to make, and Hentschel told me they had thought it would be imposing on me to ask for more. Gilbert overheard us talking about it, and said at once, "Barrington, I hope you will sing it." Of course I said I should be delighted, and Hentschel went as ambassador to Lytton on the matter, and he waived his privilege in most friendly and complimentary terms. The audience honoured me with an encore, and I sang the Captain's song from *Pinafore,* with every one in the room acting as chorus, and a fine effect it had.

Mr. McDonald Rendle, in proposing the toast of The Savoyards," made a very humorous speech, delivered in a dry manner which excited great hilarity, in which he drew comparisons between Savoy Opera and modern musical comedy "of such monumental intellectuality as, for instance, *The Belle of Mayfair*," naturally in favour of the former works, but I thought him a trifle inventive when he told us that in a village waxwork show, near a town in which the Savoy Company were playing, the proprietor, on his visit, had demonstrated his admiration of the company by labelling all his figures with the names of the different artists, and that I figured as the understudy for the "Living Skeleton."

The most notable absentee from this dinner was

poor Rosie Brandram, of whom Gilbert truly said in his speech that her only failure was "not to look like the undesirable old ladies she was doomed to play, and in spite of all the resources of the perruquier and make-up box, never appeared more than an attractive eight-and-twenty." The cause of Rosina Brandram's absence was, I believe, the illness which was soon after to prove fatal. Frank Thornton was another old comrade whom I was pleased to meet that evening, he having appeared at the first performance of *The Sorcerer*, at the Opera Comique as "the oldest inhabitant." He forsook us shortly after the Savoy was opened, and has now established himself as a popular favourite in Australia, only coming home occasionally to collect new plays for his extensive repertoire.

I was very vexed to miss the other dinner at which Gilbert was the guest of honour, given to him as recognition of the compliment paid him on receiving his knighthood. I was touring the provinces, and as I rarely see a London paper under these circumstances heard nothing of the project until too late. We used to have an annual supper of Savoyards in the old days, the chair being taken alternately by Grossmith, Cellier, and myself, and very cheery little gatherings they were, all kinds of special items being contributed both by principals and choristers. I formed a quartette for glee singing, being the alto myself, which gave us great joy—the quartette I mean. I do not quite know how it struck our audience.

Writing of audiences, is it not marvellous to notice how enormously they vary in appreciation? I have experienced a striking instance of this only lately, two nights running, during this 1908 revival of *Mikado*. An observant person being present on both might well have been excused for doubting if he or she were witnessing the same play—on the Wednesday every line securing its laugh and every number its encore, and on the Thursday practical stagnation, or perhaps I might say, comparative. How can one account for this? Of course we all know that an individual with a hearty laugh will frequently give an evening its requisite start, but can it be equally true that one person present being in the depths of gloom can affect the entire house?

An audience of one's brother and sister artists is as good and responsive a one as anybody could wish to play to, being always generous of applause, but it would not always be conducive to the maintenance of this harmonious feeling to listen to some of the criticisms made when they forgather at the close of the entertainment.

I once attended a professional matinée of *Hamlet*, given by Wilson Barrett, in which his brother George played the First Gravedigger, on conventional but very amusing lines, and on coming out heard the following conversation going on behind me: "Well, Charlie, how did you like Barrett?" "Immensely, but I didn't think much of his brother Wilson!"

I do not think audiences in London quite realize

how much it depends upon themselves whether they get full value for their money. We have been told *ad nauseam* that the actor should be unconscious of his audience, but though this may apply to a certain extent in serious plays, it cannot do so to pieces which depend for their success on the laughter they evoke, and many an artist has been discouraged for the evening by missing the first laugh which a certain speech or action has caused him to reckon upon. As an instance of the extent to which this may affect some people, I recall Gilbert telling me that on the first night of the *Mikado* he made one of his fugitive visits to the green-room, and meeting one of the company asked how the piece was going. "Fairly well," was the rather discouraging reply, which naturally distressed Gilbert considerably until meeting another of his artists, who offered the solution of such a warped view of a great success in the suggestion that the song rendered by the former artist had not been encored.

Personally I have been told that I am quite an acquisition when among the audience, having a very recognizable laugh which I am not afraid of exploiting when honestly amused. This has its merit no doubt, but on one occasion it nearly got me into trouble ; it was during the run of *Patience*, and I was suffering from a slight attack of laryngitis, which, however, was not bad enough to prevent my working and also dining with a party of friends at the Victoria Hotel. My host had taken stalls at the

Gaiety for all his guests, and argued that being really unfit to work I had better come to the play instead. He was so insistent that I gave way, sent a note round to the Savoy saying I was too ill to appear, and went off to the Gaiety. I had never done such a thing before, nor have I since, and I did not thoroughly enjoy my evening, but was stirred to laughter once, and thereby betrayed. The next morning brought me a note from Carte, hoping that I was better and ending thus, "The next time you send word you are too ill to play, don't write it on the back of a menu ; and nurse yourself at home instead of at the Gaiety Theatre." He was too kind to take any further notice of my dereliction from duty, but I felt horribly ashamed about it, and told him so.

Among the most sympathetic audiences to which I have played or sung must certainly be numbered the patients in hospital wards, an experience that I feel sure will be endorsed by all of my colleagues who have at times contributed to their amusement. This reminds me of a curious evening I once spent at a hospital for consumption not a hundred miles from Brompton. Every item which appealed to them was listened to most attentively and rapturously applauded, but when there was something they did not much care for their coughs became abominably troublesome ; the true significance of this did not dawn on me at first, but when it did my remaining contributions were given with a certain feeling of nervousness.

A well-known man of those days, E. L. Blanchard, who, under the pseudonym of " The Old Boy," used to write the pantomimes for Drury Lane, was very kind to me when I first went on the stage (this was yet another introduction which I owed to Emily Faithfull), and in addition to giving me valuable advice, would take me for occasional walks round town, his store of information rendering these little excursions most interesting. It was he who first showed me the old churchyard gate through which Dickens's " Joe " used to look, and I have never forgotten his once stopping me at a certain lamp-post opposite Charing Cross and saying, " You are now standing over the grave of Jack Sheppard."

On the occasion of a testimonial performance given to him at the Haymarket, I was much honoured by being included in the cast. The play was *Money*, and I was a servant with no lines to speak, the principal parts being played by such well-known people as Bancroft, Hare, Vezin, Neville, and Sothern, to mention only a few. This was the only time I had ever met Sothern, whom I had frequently admired, as a pittite, when playing David Garrick, and I have a faint recollection that he upset Bancroft's stolidity in one scene by introducing a gag which had something to do with a spavined horse. Oh, those visits to the pit! How I enjoyed them! More especially at the Haymarket, where it occupied the space now allotted to stalls, and where I saw

Buckstone in *The Palace of Truth*, *Pygmalion*, and *The Wicked World*, three more monuments to Gilbert's genius, which are welcome whenever seen. I have myself played in two of them, once as Pygmalion himself, in the days when I fondly imagined I had a figure, a delusion which was not shared by my old friend and critic Clement Scott, who wrote of me, "Rutland Barrington as Pygmalion looked like, and disported himself as, a prosperous butcher." There have been times when I have rather wished I had adopted that unpleasant but remunerative profession, but at the moment (though only for a moment) it rankled. I met Scott in the Strand a few days later and he crossed the street to avoid me; but I went after him, guessing the reason, and told him that I hoped I should always be able to distinguish between Clement Scott my personal friend and C.S. my critic, at which he seemed as relieved as if he had expected me to "set about him."

On another occasion I had the great pleasure of playing Chrysos in the same play with Mary Anderson as Galatea, and was very gratified to receive an offer from her to tour in America in the part. Of course I was unable to leave the Savoy, had I even wished it, but I feel sure I should have much enjoyed the experience. I have never yet been to America, but I still look forward to going there to play some day, though up to the present this has remained my only chance, which argues great remissness on the part of enterprising impresarii.

Another great favourite of my pit days, or rather nights, for the matinée was then almost unheard of, was Joseph Jefferson, whose Rip van Winkle captured all hearts with its tenderness and delightful vagabondage. I also had the good fortune to see him in farce, at the Haymarket, where he played Hugh de Brass in *Lend me Five Shillings*, and what a revelation it was of farce-acting, and what an object-lesson to many of our present-day comic men, who, it seems to me, insist too much on their points instead of endeavouring to "get home" in a quiet manner. By the way, we have at least one able exponent of the quiet method in G. P. Huntley, a countryman, I believe, of Jefferson's, which is rather curious when we consider the national reputation for "hustling." Of course there are others in this category, to name only Charles Hawtrey and James Welch, but I refer more particularly to the type known as low comedians.

XIX

THE first sport to take hold of my boy affections was, I believe, "walking the tight rope," to which I was urged by a strong desire to emulate the feat of the great Blondin, then creating a great sensation. I saw him frequently at the Crystal Palace, and nothing would satisfy me until I had rigged up a rope in our home playground, and on which I became fairly expert, so much so that I one day ventured to dance on it, with the result that I broke the rope and incidentally my head.

When walking the high rope over the fountains Blondin used to wheel a barrow full of fireworks, all of which went off at a certain spot, leaving only a row of lights along his balancing pole. One night his attendant was clumsy in taking the barrow from him (it had to be done before he could land), and to the dismay of the crowd the pole with its light was seen to fall to the ground, a distance of some hundred feet. There was a kind of gasp of horror from the thousands assembled, every one believing Blondin to have fallen; then a strong light being thrown on to the landing stage, he was observed to be hanging head down, having caught the rope by

229

one foot. The cheer that rose was enough to have made him let go, but amid a breathless silence he was observed to draw himself up to safety, when it broke out again.

After retiring from the rope-walking profession I devoted my attention to running, at which I was only a moderate success, though I still preserve a cup I won for hurdling, the race in those days being run over three hundred yards with eighteen flights. Cricket I hardly played at all until later years, we having no playground at Merchant Taylors', but when at the Savoy I took over the captaincy of the Thespians, and great fun we had. It became too expensive to keep up, however, as my team always turned up short, and I had to wire to the Oval for one or two professionals to make up. Henry Bracy, one of our tenors in *Princess Ida*, was playing for me one day at Ewell, and while we were fielding asked me if he might go into the Pavilion. On my asking him why, he told me that he wanted a "sweater," as I had put him at long-leg, where there was a terrible draught between two trees. As he possessed a very delicate voice of course I had to consent, and he did not hurry back.

Charles Glenney was playing in the same match and fielding at short-leg, when a ball came to him fairly fast, and he jumped aside. I shouted out to him, "Why didn't you stop it, Glenney?" To which he replied, "Stop it, my boy?—why, it was a whizzer!" We had no club colours in particular, and one of the members asked me to go with him and choose a blazer. Of course I went, and was rather startled when he insisted on buying, in spite of my remonstrances, an M.C.C. ribbon for his hat, an I.Z. sash, and a Guard's blazer, all of which he wore at the same time, but which failed to make of him more than a moderate cricketer. We had a most enjoyable two days' match one year at Torry Hill near Sittingbourne, between the house-party and my team of Thespians, all of us being entertained by Lord Fitzgerald. We began at noon on the Sunday, to the horror of some of the residents, as we heard afterwards. Half the countryside turned out to see the match, which, of course, aggravated the offence, as it kept many of them out of the public-houses, to the detriment of the usual Sunday trade. Golf was then in its infancy and Sunday golf unheard of, but although it has become a recognized evil, there still seems an extraordinary objection to Sunday cricket, rather reminding one of the old Euclid problems which ended with "which is absurd." There was a great effort made to establish Sunday cricket during the palmy days of the Lyric Club, which had a delightful country house at St. Ann's, Barnes, but it was not welcomed very heartily even there, though the cavillers would all take a hand at lawn tennis, and never missed the after-dinner concert or theatrical entertainments.

My last appearance at cricket was at the Oval, about 1904, when I played for the London v. Provincial Actors. I went in last but one and managed to keep my end up till time was called. I also hit a ball clean out of the ground, much to my delight, as I had announced my intention of trying to do so before going in, and we were playing well over towards the side, of course. The humorous reporter on the *Daily Mail*, in describing the incident, said that having done it I proceeded to call "Fore!" I believe I did, but it was from annoyance at not being given six for the hit. The only cricket I play now is with a soft ball at the annual fête for the Actors' Benevolent Fund at the Botanical Gardens, where we generally get badly beaten by a team of young and pretty actresses. Of course we claim that chivalry has something to say to this result, but there is no denying the skill of the Misses Statham, Billie Burke, Adrienne Augarde, Vane Featherstone, Marie Studholme, and others too numerous to mention.

Golf has become vastly more popular among actors and actresses than it was when I first started playing, some fifteen to twenty years ago, and we now number in our ranks some very fine players, notably Fred Leslie (a son of my old friend) and Herbert Ross, either of whom can hold his own in almost first-class company. I had my first lesson on the Eastbourne links one day, quite unexpectedly. The M.C.C. were playing a match in Devonshire Park, and after lunch I was starting out to watch it when Jack Russell and Smith Turberville came into the hotel, told me it was all over and that they were going golfing; would I come? With some misgivings I went, but I hit the first ball I tried and there and then fell a victim to the fascination of the game. I need hardly say I have never regretted my introduction to the finest doctor for most of the ills that flesh is heir to. Soon after this my cousin, Faithful Begg, who was then captain of Felixstowe, took me down for a week-end. We only just caught the train as it was moving off, with all my luggage still in charge of a porter on the platform. I shouted to him to throw in the clubs and never mind the rest, an order which pleased Begg immensely, as indicative of the true golfing spirit.

I have been the means of inducing many of my colleagues to take to golf, among others D'Oyly Carte and George Edwardes, the latter being for a time very keen on the game. I met him after the lapse of some weeks and he told me with great pride that he could beat Paul Rubens. I duly congratulated him, knowing nothing of Rubens's game, but the next time I met the latter, asked him about the match. He explained his defeat by the fact that on reaching each green in turn, he would ask Edwardes how many he had played, with the invariable reply, " I don't know, but I've got two for the hole."

In the autumn of 1907 I had a very pleasant day out at Gosforth Park, Newcastle, with Forbes Robertson and Roland Cunningham. There was a competition being played between local and visiting accountants, and we three followed the last couple to leave the tee. On arriving at the first green we found a photographer in waiting with his camera and I heard him ask Cunningham if we were accountants. When answered in the negative he was moving haughtily away when I felt obliged to tell him that we considered ourselves quite as interesting people but in another way, which I followed up by saying who we were. I gathered from his expression that he had not heard of Roland or myself, but he produced that day's edition of the journal he was attached to, containing an interview of Forbes Robertson, and asked if this were the man. Being satisfied on the point by Roland he followed us all round the links taking pictures. When the luncheon interval was concluded and all the gallant accountants were grouped for a picture there were no films left.

I several times tried to persuade Henry Irving to take up golf, but he seemed to think it would interfere too much with his habit of taking a siesta before acting, which he said was a necessity. He was quite surprised when I told him that I invariably slept for half an hour between golf and acting. George Alexander I have frequently golfed with, and he is no mean opponent when at his best. Tree has, I believe, only been seen on the links once, being an interested spectator of a match between Herbert Ross and another member of his company at Hoylake ; and after walking round some few holes, with a very thoughtful expression, Tree, who had watched Ross very closely, asked him, " Why do you hit it so hard ? "   I once had the pleasure of playing a round at Hoylake with the celebrated Johnny Ball, one of the most cheering opponents a man can have, full of encouragement for the new player and never winning by too great a margin.

The actors have played several matches against the county cricketers, and most enjoyable days have resulted.   My opponent has twice been the G.O.M. of cricket, Dr. W. G. Grace, a most cheery man to play with, and who keeps up a running fire of comments on the game that can be heard half a mile away.   It was most amusing once when Bosanquet and I followed the Doctor and George Edwardes at Northwood, and the discussions as to the number of strokes each had played at each hole not only lasted all the way round, but also all through lunch and most of the afternoon.

I had a narrow escape of winning a prize once at New Zealand; I had a handicap of six and went down for a day's practice the Sunday before the competition.   I had no match, and Mure Fergusson kindly took me round, giving me a third, at which odds I just managed to win.   I came down on the great day full of hope, to find to my dismay that my handicap was down to four, the result of playing the handicapper on a Sunday.

Shooting is a form of sport I never did very much of, but have some pleasant recollections of odd days in Hampshire and one day in particular in Kent, where I was one of the guests of Sir John Aird at Sutton Valence. It was a very hot "first," in fact, one of the guns went home very early in the day with a touch of sunstroke. We were walking up the birds and, at about 11.30, felt as if we had had nearly enough, when, on turning the corner of a hedgerow, we met our cheery host, followed by a servant who carried a magnum of bubbly wine. I fancy there are few men who, without being given to drink, do not keep a lively recollection of some occasion when it has been more than welcome; this was mine, and it was iced to perfection.

On the Sunday evening which concluded the visit our host unearthed from the library an old history of Kent, with the object of finding something concerning the ruins of a monastery we had all been much interested in visiting during our afternoon walk, and having found the reference he sought, proceeded to read it aloud to an attentive audience, when he suddenly came to the following · " Recent excavations point to the existence of an underground passage from the monastery to the convent which——" He stopped here abruptly, and there was a stony silence until he said, "Well, I think that will do for this evening." Every one tried hard to look unconscious, but Sir John's quaint look of confusion was too much for us, and there was a general burst of laughter. This is the only occasion I remember of a lecture on mediæval customs proving humorous.

Coarse fishing was a very favourite pastime of mine, and, having heard whispers of large fish of some sort in the lake near the house, I went forth one day and captured what I thought was a carp of about six pounds. I took it to be set up and called the next day to arrange about it. The taxidermist told me he had put it in his goldfish tank overnight to keep it fresh, and it had come to life and eaten all his goldfish. There was no doubt about its being alive, though how it had survived the journey from Maidstone on the speedy Chatham and Dover railway was a mystery to me. Tench must be hardy fellows.

There is a somnolent excitement about punt-fishing on the Thames which I used to find very attractive, and in those days it was possible to get some good sport. Spending a holiday one summer at Medmenham, I was fishing from the bank one day with my wife, when a skiff full of people went by rather near us; after passing I heard the man pulling stroke inform the lady steering who I was, whereupon she remarked, " Never ! Why I thought he was a much younger man." This amused my wife immensely, in fact until late in the afternoon, when a steam launch crowded with " trippers " passed by, and one man said to his friend, " Bill, twig the girl on the bank fishing?" Bill replied, after a steady look, " Girl? Where d'you find your old women ?" I made no remark, but the balance was restored.

Lawn tennis of course claimed me as a victim

at one time, and I developed a quite useful "garden-party" form, owing in a great measure to the opportunities I had of playing with the Renshaws, Lawford, and other stars of the arena at Forbes Winslow's place at Hammersmith, and also on the lawns of Harry Chinnery's lovely retreat near Teddington Weir. I once had the audacity to enter for the championship at Wimbledon, and actually survived the first round. I fancy I was encouraged to do this by the form I displayed in a foursome at Datchet, when I had George Grossmith as my partner against Henry Kemble and Corney Grain. The match was left unfinished owing to Grain striking himself violently on the nose with his racquet and retiring using language about the game. It was during this visit of his to Grain that Kemble was run to earth by the income-tax collector, a person whom actors are, I believe, fairly successful in eluding (and with reason I think), and he said, "Well, I will pay you this time, but you must tell Her Majesty that she must not look on me as a permanent source of income!"

My last game of lawn tennis, after an abstention of at least ten years, owing to the superior attraction of golf, was played in August, 1906, at Wimbledon with Gordon Cleather and two others. It was the day of the production of *Amāsis*, and I wanted a distraction for the mind. I found four setts quite enough, one of them taking fourteen games to decide, but it put me in great form for the evening.

Racing has always had a great fascination for me, and for years I never missed the two Epsom meetings. I saw the great race for the Gold Cup between Bend Or and Robert the Devil, practically a match, as there were no other runners. I was on the hill and had my modest investment on the winner, Bend Or, but when I went to collect my money I stood lost in wonder. Where were the rows of bookmakers who had been driving a roaring trade on both horses at evens? I never saw such a clearance in my life; there were dozens of little trumpery stands lying about and no sign of the pencillers, with the exception of some half-dozen well-known and solid men, with whom it is always safe to bet, but with whom on that occasion I of course had not invested.

Newmarket I have only attended once, but it was a memorable visit for several reasons. My first sensation on arriving on the course was that here at last was a meeting at which we could be contented to "look on" without having a bet, but that impression wore off after a couple of races.

The most important reason for remembering the visit was this: that on the way to racing, after a late breakfast, I proceeded to issue to my host and his friends a list of what I termed "Barrington's finals." Needless to say, they all lost, but it gave me an idea which materialized on the way back to town in the train. I wrote what I fondly hoped was a humorous description of my day's doings, signed it with the *nom-de-plume* of "Lady Gay" (it was written from a feminine point of view), and sent it off to my old friend Burnand, the editor of *Punch*, with a note asking, "Any good to you?" To my great surprise and delight I received, by return post, proofs for correction. This developed into a weekly contribution which ran for nearly a year, so that I almost feel I was once on the staff of *Punch*. I am not aware of the full extent of the consequent increase in the circulation, but I bought a copy myself every week while it lasted.

I had an interesting racing experience in connection with the late Duke of Beaufort and a celebrated mare he owned called Rêve d'Or. She was entered at Sandown for a five-furlong sprint, a considerably shorter distance than that she was accustomed to, and, if I remember right, the famous horseman Tom Cannon rode her. I met the Duke in the paddock, and he stopped to exchange a few words with me. We naturally spoke of the mare, and he told me she was in the best of health, but he feared the distance was not far enough for her. Having made my small bet I thought I would see the race from a spot about two-thirds of the way home, so strolled across to the rails. Rêve d'Or, as usual, began slowly, and Cannon soon commenced to bustle her along. I was watching intently through my glasses, and just before they came past me I fancied that I could see the mare suddenly realize that she had not so far to go as usual and must hurry up. She immediately began to put in her best work, and if this story were fiction would of course have won, but being fact she was just beaten a head. That same night I again met the Duke and told him what I thought I had seen, and he confirmed my impression by telling me exactly where I must have stood, as he himself had, unknown to both of us, been close by and had read the story of the race in the same way, having noticed Rêve d'Or's expression.

Of course all of us at Daly's took a great interest in "The Chief's" horses, especially Santoi, who decorated his sideboard with some very handsome cups.

Racing is his great relaxation, and I think he is never so happy as when "one of his" has "rolled home," and all his friends have been put on the good thing. Naturally these "good things" do not always materialize, and I remember a terrible afternoon at Windsor when we drove over, a family wagonette full, from Winkfield. He had four horses running, and the wagonette had a dash on each of the first three and nothing on the fourth, who had been "off his feed for some days" and was the only one that won. In addition to this bad luck, I had a very narrow escape of having my face (such as it is) spoilt for life. I was discussing with a friend in the paddock the merits of the horses as they were being led round, when he suddenly grabbed my arm and pulled me back about a yard, shouting, "Look out!" The horse just passing us had lashed out, and his hoof knocked the cigar out of my mouth and just

Q

touched me on the chest. Since then I have been careful to walk on the "led" side of a horse, and I think I never before so keenly appreciated the value of a yard.

I have one racing and cricket combined reminiscence which was also connected with a horse belonging to the late Duke of Beaufort, called Eastern Emperor. I had, "on information received," backed it to win something over a hundred for the Royal Hunt Cup, at fairly long odds, for which, on the day of the race, I could see very excellent hedging, *but*, I had also backed a bill for a friend of mine who had exercised the usual prerogative of friendship in leaving me to meet his liability, and the amount for which I had backed the horse would just cover it if it won, so I naturally determined on the bold policy of "all or none."

I had at that time never been to Ascot and had no great desire to go, in addition to which the Thespians had an important match at Buckhurst Hill, which to me was a far greater attraction. In the excitement of the match I forgot all about the race, and as we were leaving the ground some one appeared with an evening paper. Even then I felt uninterested until I heard a bystander ask, "What won the Hunt Cup?" I then listened breathlessly for the answer, which was "Eastern Emperor," when, to the astonishment of my team, I threw into the air a brand-new bowler hat I was wearing and proceeded to kick it out of shape. Then

I had an uneasy feeling as to whether I should be paid; I was, however, and so was the bill, but my friend has never paid me.

This is an argument against the supposed wisdom of hedging which I can support by another case, that of Hackness's Cambridgeshire, over which I stood to win about sixty to nothing, but I had "laid" the mare with a friend, and in my ignorance, having omitted to give the bookmaker's name for the money, found myself in the unenviable position of having to pay without receiving, the said bookmaker being one of several who were severely knocked over the race in question.

I do not quite know if dancing comes under the head of "sport," but it is certainly exercise, especially stage dancing, of which I have done a fair amount.   There is a dance in *Pinafore*, in which the First Lord, the Captain, and Josephine take part, which is very effective when done with energy.

One night I observed sitting in a box a lady whom I was anxious to impress with my charm as a dancer; I was going very strong—indeed, as she told me afterwards, she was in the act of pointing out to her companion my obvious grace—when I tried an extra twirl, my feet went up in the air, and down I came on the deck—a blow to my vanity, to say nothing of the deck.

In the present revival (1908) my dance is, I am told, as graceful as of yore, but I am taking no risks.

XX

How interesting it should be, I have often thought, to make a collection of little items and queer points which stick in the memories of playgoers in connection with all the different plays and players they have seen, and what a bizarre collection it would prove.

By way of a personal contribution to any such would-be collector, I offer this chapter of odd remembrances of things seen and heard which, for reasons which may or may not be clear, have established a permanent lodgment in my memory.

It is a moot point how many playgoers interest themselves in a careful perusal of the programme before the commencement of the play; of course, a large percentage of those who do so would be found among the occupants of the unreserved seats, these having little else to employ the time of waiting; but that many of the other occupants of the house do not do so is frequently evident from the stage in a general and hurried consultation of the document on the appearance of some player, possibly so well made up as to defy recognition, or deputizing for some popular favourite.

Photograph W. H. Midwinter & Co.

FRANÇOIS CELLIER.

Personally, I make a practice of reading all matter connected with the play in the case of musical pieces before the curtain rises, my experience having taught me the possibility of gathering as clear an idea of the plot in this way as any other. But when the play is a comedy, drama, or farce, I much prefer to remain in ignorance, as far as possible, as to who is playing the different characters, finding very often as the result of this plan an increase of enjoyment consequent upon the natural maintenance of the illusion.

A striking example of this was afforded me lately in witnessing *The White Man*, many of the characters in which were played by Americans whose names I do not even now know, in spite of three visits to the play, which I found perfectly fascinating from the end of the first act to its conclusion.

The contrasted alertness and stolidity of the cowboys and the touching submission and pathos of the little squaw were most delightful, and the intense feeling expressed by her, wordlessly, must live in the memory of many who saw this artistic performance.

The charm of the whole thing impressed me so strongly that one day when in Shipwright's my tonsorial artist pointed out to me a customer who he said was " Big Bill " the cowboy overseer, I resolutely declined to look at him, though I would have done so with great pleasure had he been dressed for the part.

Another example of "illusion maintained" occurred some years ago when the famous Salvini came to astonish and please London with a fine performance of *Othello*.

The play was so well acted all round that even the most superficial acquaintance with Italian was hardly necessary to one's enjoyment, and I have never forgotten the effect of one short speech, by the Emilia of the cast, which rang through the house with its intensity—"Aita! Aita! El moro ha assassinato Desdemona!"

The occasion was a "Professional Matinée" given by Salvini, and it was amusing to listen to the "views" of some of my colleagues in the vestibule between the acts, one fairly celebrated tragedian tempering his praise with the statement, "All the same, it is hardly *my* idea of Othello"; to which his listener replied, "No, of course not"; but the irony passed unobserved.

From grave to Gaiety is a natural transition, but in considering the type of piece associated with this theatre of late years, one cannot help the feeling that but for a change of title and locale it might be the same play all the time.

In the halcyon days of Nellie Farren and Fred Leslie, Royce and others, there seemed to be more backbone in the pieces, but I would not go so far as to say they were more amusing; and Payne has certainly been a tower of strength for many years, his marked capability in varying his method and his capacity for inventing humorous little details being strong factors in his success.

One such item recurs to me as affording one of the heartiest laughs I remember. The play was *The Orchid*, and after a long search for the missing bloom, he saw it suddenly on a hand-barrow, stalked it in the manner of a butterfly catcher, using his hat as the net! A small thing perhaps, but only another proof of the fact that one never knows what is going to "get home."

In this connection who could have imagined that *Miss Hook of Holland* would achieve such a lengthy run? It was certainly a wholesome if somewhat innocuous evening's entertainment, and undoubtedly owed most of its fascination to the excellent band of comedians, Huntley, Barrett, and Gracie Leigh, but my most vivid recollection is that of the 'sleepy" man, whom I shrewdly suspect of being invented by one of the comedians.

It was in this piece that I first saw and admired Elsie Spain, little dreaming that I should shortly stand *in loco parentis* to her in *Pinafore*.

Two pistols are an odd remembrance to have of a play, but so it happens to be in the case of an adaptation of Wilkie Collins's *The Woman in White*, which I saw many years ago at the Olympic, with Vining in the part of the scheming scoundrel Fosco, whose only weakness appeared to be a fondness for canaries.

He was chirruping to his cageful with his back

to a pair of folding doors, which opened silently to show the faces of two men holding pistols, which they pointed at him. Of course, he turned round in the nick of time, but he was eventually shot "off," which disappointed me considerably; had he been shot "on" I might never have been haunted with two pistols.

I used to frequent the Royalty as much as possible in the days of those two incomparable comedians, Didier and Schey, seeing, among other plays, *Tricoche et Cacolet, La Boule*, and *Le Réveillon* (?).

These two actors were yet another proof of the value of contrast, not only from a physical but also artistic point of view, and I think I never saw two comedians play into each other's hands better.

My recollection in this instance is of the entire company in the piece seated at supper, for quite a long scene, and the servant bringing round the wine with great regularity, and with equal regularity finding Schey's glass empty, until on his last round, when murmuring "Chambertin ou Chateau Larose, Monsieur?" he was met with the request, "Tous les deux, mon ami—tous les deux!"

The ease with which this supper party was managed I only remember to have seen once equalled, which was when *The Man from Blankney's* was played at the Haymarket, and I had the pleasure of supplying Charlie Hawtrey with one of the little stories out of which he made such capital at the table.

I was greatly interested in both Hawtrey and Titheradge in *The Message from Mars*, and out of the haze of admiration excited by their performance, stands the startling effect of the sudden disappearance of Hawtrey's fur overcoat and other spruce garments, leaving him in the rags of a tramp! Of course, I know how it was done, but the fact remains—it stuck—though the clothes did not, fortunately.

Charles Mathews furnished many a delightful evening for me at the old Gaiety Theatre years ago, and I well remember a little bit of "business" which he invariably used when taking a "call" at the conclusion of *Cool as a Cucumber*; he would stroll on in front of the curtain in his imperturbable manner, bow, place a finger on the pulse of his left hand, and express facially his delight at being at last "greatly moved."

The palmy days of the Lyceum found me a frequent visitor, especially when drama was the fare provided, and my recollections of Irving are many and various.

By the way, these recollections date further back than that, in fact to his performance of Digby Grand in *The Two Roses* at the Vaudeville, which I believe I am correct in thinking of as his first great London success.

I admired him greatly in *The Lyons Mail* and the *Corsican Brothers*, at the first night of which it was my privilege to be present. Pinero also played in this piece, and, when made up, so nearly resembled Irving that for a moment he captured the reception intended for the great man, who entered later on in the play. The mistake was soon discovered and produced a universal but thoroughly good-natured laugh.

Irving and Terriss, who played Château Renaud very finely, being both excellent fencers, gave us in the duel scene the finest fight I have ever seen, ending in a dramatic and almost nerve-destroying manner. The "thrill" of it was enhanced by its being fought in falling snow of so realistic a nature that the combatants brushed it out of their way with their feet before commencing.

Of course, this was burlesqued at the Gaiety by Nellie Farren and Royce, the former stopping the fight because all the snow fell on Royce, and insisting on having her share.

In the final scene where the ghost appears to thank his brother for having revenged him, much hilarity was provoked by the appearance of at least six ghosts of different sizes and shapes!

I believe it is on record that the sedate audiences at the Lyceum were more than once upset by the presence among them of spectators who had unwisely seen the burlesque *first*.

At the Vaudeville I also saw in those days the finest all-round performance of *The School for Scandal* that I imagine has ever been "presented," which is not wonderful when the cast contained

William Farren, Henry Neville, John Clayton, Tom Thorne, David James (I think), and a delightful Lady Teazle in Amy Faucet. I cannot imagine a better Charles and Joseph Surface than Henry Neville and poor Clayton, an old schoolfellow of mine, whose career was all too short.

I forget who the Careless of this occasion was, but mention of the play reminds me of a story in connection with the part, told of Sothern in his early days, but for the truth of which I cannot vouch, though it seems to me sufficiently *ben trovato* to be worth repeating.

Sothern did not sing, and rather than have the song cut it was arranged that he should sit at the top of the table, close to the back cloth of the scene, behind which a singer was concealed, while Sothern acted and mouthed the song.

It was a great success, and Sothern sat down delighted, only to find to his horror that the audience insisted on an encore! He turned his head to the hole cut in the cloth behind him and whispered anxiously, "Are you there?"—No answer!—He then bowed gracefully to the audience, coughed, put his hand on his throat deprecatingly and sat down. Meantime the singer had been hurriedly summoned, and just as Sothern was proceeding with the dialogue the first few strains of "Here's to the maiden" floated through the orifice!

Still another example of the value of physical and artistic contrast was presented by Wyndham and

Hill in the old days of farce at the Criterion, the vivacity of Wyndham in such plays as *Where's the Cat?* and *Brighton* (a vivacity which remains with him when requisite even to this day, as witness his last revival of *The Candidate*), finding its complement in the stolid figure and humour of Hill, and later on also in his successor Blakeley, whose humour was of the same rich type.

There was a clever adaptation of *Bébé* also given at the Criterion, in which Lottie Venne scored a great success (by no means an unusual accomplishment for her), and I distinctly recollect the angry manner in which she brushed a silk hat, to the distress of its owner and most men in the stalls. This great little artist possesses, in addition to her many charms, a wonderful manner of speaking that kind of doubtful line which is sometimes alluded to by journalists as "skating on thin ice"; and this power was occasionally abused by authors, much to her distress. She once came to me at rehearsal and pointing out a speech said, "B. dear, I can't say that, now, can I?" My obvious reply was, "Well, Lottie, if you can't, no one can." The line was spoken, and as spoken by her did not attract the attention she feared.

At Toole's Theatre I once saw a most amusing piece of the burlesque order, in which Edouin and Lionel Brough were both playing, the former as a Heathen Chinee (a wonderful performance) and the latter as a kind of freebooter, who carried a large bag, into which he dropped anything portable which he found lying about.

The night I was present there was an Eton boy in the stage box whose laughter was so frequent and so loud as to occasionally distract the attention of the audience.   After one unusually hearty outburst Brough set the house in a roar by saying, "If any one will hand me up that young gentleman I will put him in the bag!"

Several times I saw Toole play Caleb Plummer, a part to which he gave a pathetic touch which was wholly delightful.   The dominant recollection I have of him is the expression of artistic pride with which he painted round spots of a brilliant red on the little wooden horses in the toy shop.

What an unwise thing it is to correct a mistake one may have made in a speech ; it is quite an even chance that few, if any, have noticed the slip, and to correct it is to draw attention.   At the Vaudeville I once saw Walter Montgomery play Claude in *The Lady of Lyons ;* he was a charming romantic actor and quite the idol of the softer sex of his day.   The Pauline was down in the programme thus, "Pauline —by an Amateur," although it appeared hardly necessary to emphasize the fact.   However, she was doing fairly well until she informed the audience tragically that "my father is on the bank of verge-ruptcy," corrected herself, and upset everybody's seriousness.

I went to the Lyceum once to see a play in which

Irving shot Clayton dead, but on the night of my visit, to the dismay of every one, the gun missed fire! Irving tried it again; no use; and things seemed to be at a deadlock, with John Clayton walking about the stage passively waiting to be killed for what seemed like ten minutes, until Irving solved the difficulty by clubbing the gun and felling him with it, but as of course he could not really touch him, it was hardly as realistic a death as it might have been.

Writing of drama reminds me of one of its finest exponents, in the person of Geneviève Ward, whose performance in *Forget-me-not* was most impressive. There is a situation in which she sees outside a window a man who is there avowedly for the purpose of killing her; we even see the dagger in his hand; and she unsuccessfully implores her husband (I think it is) not to turn her out of the house. He, not knowing of the fate awaiting her, orders her out, and I shall never forget the force with which she played the scene and the awful expression with which she went to certain death by violence. In striking contrast to this was her expression at our last meeting, when she sat next to me " on the Bench " when I played the Judge in *Trial by Jury*, with whom she flirted to such an extent as to almost upset the " business " flirtation with the fair plaintiff.

At the Globe in the old days I saw a play called, I believe, *The Looking Glass*, in which Shine gave an excellent performance of a vulgarian proprietor of the newspaper from which the play took its title.

Tree played a foreign prince of the "adventurer" type, and was much worried by an aristocratic dame (played, I believe, by Rose Leclerc), who carried a toy dog about with her. I have never forgotten Tree's expression on the frequent occasions when she handed him the little beast, saying, "Prince, would you hold Horace?" A later impression of Tree is in *The Beloved Vagabond*, where he performed such marvellous feats of beer drinking as fairly astonished the audience. I have not met him since, but am longing for the opportunity to ask if he used a trick glass; if not, the ordeal must have been severe.

There is a type of comedian which, for want of a better word, I might describe as "untiring," whose vivacity and restlessness appeals very strongly to a huge section of the public, though I am happy to think there is an equally large following for the "reposeful" style, amongst which I must number a friend of my own who took me to see a play in which a well-known and popular exponent of the untiring method was appearing. While I devoted my best attention to the strenuosities of the entertainment he slept peacefully throughout the evening. Of one of the reposeful denomination, Weedon Grossmith, I have a recollection in connection with Pinero's play *The Amazons*, at the Court Theatre. Weedon played a dyspeptic nobleman, and I well remember the hectic flush he assumed, combined with the highly depressed expression of face, with which he delivered the line, "*We* ought never to take tea!"

Some years ago there occurred the periodical out-cry of pessimism concerning the work of the modern play-writer as compared with the " grand old dramas " of our forefathers' time, and Hollings-head, who then presided over the fortunes of the Gaiety Theatre, decided, by way of proving the case in favour of the moderns, to produce one or two of the much-vaunted antique successes.

I saw the first, and, if I remember aright, the series stopped at that, which was not wonderful, as the most thrilling and blood-curdling situations excited uproarious laughter, culminating in the escape of the hero from prison, guarded by some dozen or so sentries, who carefully went to sleep *en masse* while he climbed the wall by means of iron clamps which were evidently a permanent part of the structure. The gentleman in question announced at the com-mencement of the scene that he had been some five years in the dungeon "without food"! so that his original strength must have been abnormal.

XXI

THE moment I heard that the ban had been removed from the *Mikado*, I had a premonition that
Pooh Bah would revisit the scene of his former
triumph. Pleasant presentiments have an unpleasant
habit of rarely materializing, but in this case it
proved a correct one, and the following letter greeted
me one morning in April (not the 1st) :—

" DEAR MR. BARRINGTON,
     " If you would like to have a quiet run
through of your music, Mr. Cellier will be very glad
to meet you at the Savoy at eleven o'clock on Tuesday.   " Yours sincerely,
                              " HELEN CARTE."

This was an invitation amounting almost to a
Royal Command, and needless to say, I did "like,"
and duly presented myself at the time indicated.
The very time, eleven, was a link with the past, the
modern call being rarely fixed for anything earlier
than noon, and many artists even then being half an
hour late; but my old training stood me in good
stead, and without the semblance of an effort I was

there on the stroke of time. There was another
victim present at this portentous "voice trial" in the
person of my old young friend Harry Lytton, who
was as anxious to qualify for the part of the Mikado
as I was for Pooh Bah. We were both, I fancy,
highly nervous and horribly afraid of François Cellier,
our kindly musical director, for the reason that he
carries in his brain-cells every note of these operas as
written by Sullivan, and is charmingly intolerant of
the slightest deviation from the score of the maestro.
In support of this he told me a story at this very
rehearsal concerning a well-known tenor who was
engaged to play Ivanhoe alternately with Ben Davies,
the originator of the part; Cellier was sitting in the
stalls with Sullivan at the tenor's first rehearsal, and
at the close of one scene where he should have
finished piano, in order to allow the *Ivanhoe* "motif"
to receive full value at the hands of the magnificent
orchestra, the tenor introduced a B flat, which he
hung on to as we all know tenors do. Cellier jumped
up from his seat, and turning to Sullivan exclaimed
loudly, "My God, did you hear that?" it being to
his mind nothing less than sacrilege. Sullivan appeared a trifle embarrassed and said, "Don't worry,
Frank; I told him he might do it; but if you don't
approve I will speak to him about it." François, of
course, could say no more, but to his great joy the
tenor told him later that, "thanks to you, I am
robbed of my B flat." Although I had no desire to
emulate this feat, and as I do not possess the note

the reason is obvious, I was quite unnerved by the tale, but proceeded to do my best; I had ventured to take with me as a kind of "reserve" my old friend Major Gunston, who had been present at the original production of the *Mikado,* and who had very kindly definitely promised to remove me should he see signs of the strain becoming too great, and see to it that I recuperated in due form in the Café Parisien; but even he was so overcome by the solemnity of the occasion and the Gilbert-and-Sullivan atmosphere which pervaded the stage as to remain oblivious not only of the lapse of time, but also, *mirabile dictu,* of the imperative necessity for eating and drinking. However, both Lytton and myself passed the test triumphantly, and Cellier having promised (provided I would have a good hour at the music before the next rehearsal) to put in a good word for us with Mrs. Carte, all ended happily and we unbent in company at lunch.

Of course it was inevitable that I should have forgotten odd bits of my music, and in one number I finished a good half-bar in front of the accompanist, which caused Cellier to remind me of a piece in which I played at the Opera Comique called *After All,* in which I had a patter-song to sing, and on one occasion at a benefit, with a strange conductor, I came to the end of the song long before the band, and to Cellier's delight, remarked loudly, "I won." Of course, it was not Sullivan's music, or his delight would have been tempered with horror.

For about a week we frolicked (reverently) through our preliminary rehearsals by way of getting into some sort of form before the advent of the author, and then arrived the momentous day. At eleven-thirty on Monday, April 13, 1908, Sir William Gilbert made his first appearance as a titled stage manager, and it was soon made evident that the master mind is as alert and keen as ever, and those of us who were uncertain as to what is " gag " and what is "original" in our parts were feeling slightly nervous. That there was no need for this feeling was soon apparent, for there was a geniality about the proceedings which formed a welcome contrast to the north-east wind which was blowing in the Strand, and had given us all a jaundiced view of rehearsals and work generally. I had made a virtuous resolve to do without my " book " at this rehearsal, but, from what cause I cannot guess, I could not remember one speech correctly, and worse than all felt as if I never should. Of course this feeling wore off, and all kinds of little bits of business kept recurring to me, but even then I had not recovered everything by the first night and have been reminded of some since. In one situation where Pitti Sing, now played by that delightful little artist Jessie Rose, puts herself forward in place of Yum-Yum, Gilbert did not like the " business," and when told by the stage manager that it was the original way of doing it, appealed to me for confirmation, which I was able to give, where-upon he remarked, " Oh, it's classic, is it ?   Well, we must not interfere with the classics." On the other hand several such introductions of a more modern growth have been sternly suppressed, with much advantage to the piece. It has been Sir William's aim in this revival to get as near to the original rendering as possible, but it is not always easy to separate the old from the new, especially when some of the artists have been playing the parts at intervals for so long a time.

I renewed my acquaintance with "Simpson's" during these rehearsals, in company with Gilbert, and although some of the homeliness of the place has disappeared owing to its new and gorgeous decoration, it was very pleasant to find the same waiters and carvers in attendance, the same excellent joints at our disposal, almost the same appetite to enjoy them with, and absolutely the same type of people frequenting the restaurant that I remember twenty years ago; indeed, I believe if not the identical people, they are sons and daughters who worthily maintain the old traditions of "'Simpson's' before a matinée."

At length we arrived at the first night of our revival of *Mikado*, and what an excitement there was; the pit and gallery had been filled for hours, in fact since about five o'clock, and Mrs. Carte had very kindly sent them in tea and bread and butter. They passed the time away by singing, led by a girl with a very sweet voice, all the songs and concerted numbers from the whole series of Savoy Operas, carefully abstaining, with excellent taste, from giving anything from the *Mikado*.

On taking his seat to conduct the overture, Cellier was received almost as if he were the composer, a public recognition of the well-known fact how much his heart is in his work ; and then the other receptions ; the warmth of my own brought a feeling of chokiness that very nearly prevented me from delivering my first lines. Workman, Lytton, and in fact all the cast were scarcely less warmly greeted, and the scene at the end of the evening was strongly reminiscent of the same scene twenty odd years ago, though to some of us, either side of the curtain, the pleasure was tempered with the sorrow of missing so many old friends. Both the stage and the auditorium seem to me on some evenings peopled with ghosts of those I have seen there so often.

We had a rather funny experience about a week after opening, in the way of artists forgetting their parts, in fact it was a little epidemic. It began with Lytton misplacing a word, then Workman fell over a speech, I cut something, Nanki Poo omitted an entire line, and in the number immediately following the bassoon went wrong ; he was a deputy, and when the encore came Cellier looked anxiously towards him, and the *clarinette* made signs that he had put the bassoon right, but while doing so forgot to take up his own cue, which so disturbed Cellier that he omitted to beat the time. All this sounds like a terrible fiasco, but in reality was only noticeable to the initiated, amongst whom must be included the well-known performer on the drums, Henderson (who was with us at the Opera Comique), who thoroughly enjoyed the situation.

Some of our most frequent patrons are children, who are brought to our matinées in great numbers and who seem to me somehow to know the piece. This may be so in truth, for in one case, during the last revival, Sir Lewis McIver told me that his wife had been used to telling her little ones the story of Yum-Yum and Nanki Poo as if it were a fairy tale, and their excitement when they were brought to see the real thing was immense, all the characters as they appeared being greeted with affectionate recognition. We also have frequent visitors from Japan among our audiences, but they, naturally, do not excite the attention that was bestowed on a boxful of little ladies in kimonos from the Japanese village at Knightsbridge in 1885, who I expect did not understand a single word of what was said or sung.

One point strikes me almost nightly, and that is the way in which the dialogue "goes"; many of the phrases have been adopted as everyday colloquialisms, and yet when delivered on a stage excite the same laughter as before; no little compliment this to the master mind which invented them. The most important up-to-date alteration made has been the addition of an encore verse to Koko's song, "I've got a little list," and this has provoked a rather curious experience. Workman was unable to learn it in time for the first night, and when he did try it, a few nights later, came to hopeless grief in the latter part of it. We were talking this over and then discussed the merit of the verse, which both of us had the temerity to describe as "not very good"; however, not having an alternative, he persevered with it, and, to our mutual amusement, the first night he got the full value of it he could easily have taken another encore. We have both (silently) apologized to Gilbert for our obtuseness.

It was a great gratification to me to read the dictum of one critic to the effect that "he sings his music with delightful assumption of the vocal mannerisms of a certain age." I am not absolutely sure whether this is a veiled allusion to my tale of years, or meant to refer to a species of tenor production which I adopt at intervals with a certain effect, but in either case, as I say, it gratifies me almost as much as it appears to amuse my hearers.

A good deal of praise has been apportioned in the present revival to the good work on the part of the choristers, and though well deserved this is scarcely to be wondered at, when considering that many of the choristers of both sexes have played parts in the operas. It is indeed a tribute to their loyalty to the management that with perfect equanimity they will play a part one week and sing chorus the next, the reward being a steady engagement with a manageress whose interest in their welfare is as strong as in that of herself and the plays.

To have been an "old Savoyard," that is to say, one of the original company, seems to confer not only a great measure of dignity but, in the minds of some, a greater natural activity in old age. This was clearly proved to me some few nights after the *Mikado* revival by the visit of a friend to my dressing-room. He told me he was sitting in the last row of the stalls and immediately behind him there were two dear old ladies renewing their former acquaintance with the play. At the end of the encores for the " Flowers that bloom in the spring," one of them said to the other, " Look at that wonderful Mr. Barrington dancing like that." " Lovely !" said the other. " But why is it so wonderful, dear ? " To which number one replied, " Don't you know ? Why, he's well over seventy ! "

Apropos the extraordinary fact that you can accomplish feats on the stage which might be impossible without the stimulus of an audience, I have heard it stated as a fact that during the last few months that Buckstone played, although driven to the theatre in a four-wheeler and assisted up the stairs to his room and from there to the stage by his valet, once on the boards he was able to give the necessary spring to enable him to sit on a table and swing his feet. All the same I found the first week rather trying when it came to rolling about on the stage, and at an early rehearsal, when Gilbert remarked rather doubtfully, " Barrington, can you ' go down ' in the way you used to ? " and having confidently replied " Oh yes," I proceeded to demonstrate that I could, I found it more difficult than I antici pated, but I have since become quite acclimatized.

In July, 1908, comes my first experience of a "repertoire," in the shape of a revival of *Pinafore*, which we are now playing on alternate nights with the *Mikado*.

This opera, naturally, did not require as much rehearsal as many of them, being so short as to necessitate a first piece being played, and as Sir William was at the same time busily engaged rehearsing *Rosencrantz* and *Guildenstern* (in which he also played the King), he was only occupied in polishing up our brasswork for a little over a week.

It was almost as great a night as the *Mikado* revival, and I have an impression that it is " new " to many more people than is the Japanese piece.

That it was not new to some of the " galleryites," and most particularly to one man amongst them, I had ample and personal experience on the first and second nights.

Gilbert had introduced a line into my part which might be, and was, construed into a reference to the present "strained relations" existing between certain well-known and deservedly popular naval officers of high position, and the line was received with mingled laughter and " booing," some few cries of " Author ! Author ! " and from one stentorian voice the remark, " Stick to the book ! "

It is manifestly unfair to visit the sins (?) of the

author on the actor, and might have been somewhat distressing to an artist with a less phlegmatic
temperament than Captain Corcoran; but, of course,
it is quite possible that if a reproof was intended it
was meant for the author, in which case I for one
still less can understand the justice of it, for surely
the man who wrote the piece has the right to alter
or add to his work if he wishes!

This argument, however, would not seem to hold
good with these Savoy classics, and Gilbert himself,
when giving me the line, said something to the effect
that "the Press will very likely object to it, Barrington."

It was quite like old times to read that I "occasionally failed to *quite* reach some of my top notes,"
a fact of which I was quite conscious, as I also was
of a bad attack of bronchitis, which rendered me
absolutely breathless after three encores for the
dancing number, "Ring the merry bells," which is
followed (without leaving the stage) by a heavy
duet with Deadeye and a stormy scene with the
eloping couple!

There is another reason why some of Sullivan's
music is difficult to sing, which may appeal perhaps
more strongly to musical connoisseurs than to the
average listener, and that is that should he require
the bass line in a quartette and there is no bass on
the stage the tenor has to do his best with it, and
vice versa, while a poor baritone is expected to sing
everything that comes his way.

This is more noticeable, naturally, in his one or two earlier works, and the part of Captain Corcoran is liberally sprinkled with D's, E flats, and even G's.

In spite of these small drawbacks the revival is an eminently popular one, and, as Gilbert himself remarked, "one of the best he has had both from an acting and a singing point of view." Something of this is due to our new soprano, Elsie Spain, whose method is quite Savoyard; and to Dick Deadeye Harry Lytton imparts a touch of pathos which is extremely effective. Workman is naturally an excellent Sir Joseph Porter, a part which he has had time to mature to great advantage, but it is extraordinary how I miss the magnificent attenuation in figure of my old comrade, George Grossmith.

Apropos this revival I had a bet of sixpence with Cellier that at the first rehearsal taken by Gilbert he would not commence work until he had pointed out that one of the ropes was in wrong position. Cellier asked, "Which one?" But not having Sir William's nautical knowledge I could only answer, "I don't know, but *some* one." The bet was made and I won it.

After a week of *Pinafore* it seemed very strange to be playing the *Mikado* again, and I wondered very much how many people in the audience had come to see *Pinafore* without duly consulting the advertisements, and whether they were at all disappointed.

The song to the moon, at the commencement of Act II, was "hardly ever" sung by me, even in the old days, the only effect to be got with it being a vocal one, and therefore rather out of my line. I should feel more at home were it of a patter or topical kind; but to suggest such an alteration would make a certainty of something worse than "boiling oil" for all concerned, and the wiser course seems to be to leave it out.

The facsimile letter below was written by Gilbert when returning me the proofs of this chapter, and humorously sums up the situation as regards interpolations in his operas.

EPILOGUE

AND so ends a task which I commenced with great diffidence, have pursued with great pleasure, and concluded with relief.

If but a tithe of my pleasure is transmitted to my readers as the result of wading through these pages, I am more than satisfied.

In compiling the work I have at least refuted the accusation of my old friend Gilbert in his "Foreword," that I have "an underlying principle never to do anything for myself that I can induce others to do for me," as every word has been written by me, and not even dictated, so that to myself alone will attach any blame or praise which it may evoke.

Some of the responsibility, however, may belong to Mr. Lloyd Williams, the genial editor of *Black and White*, who was the first to propose that I should contribute certain articles to his paper, for the embodiment of which in this book I am gratefully indebted.

Finally I promise that I will never do it again, or at least, should great pressure be applied, "hardly ever"!